That's Deep.

That's Deep.

A Mindfulness Guide for College Students

Lule West

Exact Rush

Exact Rush Multimedia Publishing
Exact Rush, LLC.
353 W. Greensboro Ct.
Boise, ID 83706

Exact Rush Multimedia Publishing and the Exact Rush logo are trademarks of Exact Rush, LLC.

Cover Design: Ivan Gatski

Cover Image © Grace Burns

Cataloging-in-Publication Data is on file at the Library of Congress

ISBN: 979-8-9898235-0-5

Contents

Chapter Three: Treat Yo'Self   89

Chapter Four: IYKYK   119

Chapter Five: Situationships 147

Chapter Six: What's Your Zodiac? 179

Chapter Seven: Levelin' Up — 213

Common Challenges — 239

Authors — 247

Audio Exercises — 252

Introduction

What's So Deep?

Embracing Mindfulness

By picking up this book, you've taken a significant step towards enhancing your well-being and unlocking a more centered, peaceful version of yourself. In these pages, you'll discover how mindfulness can help you navigate challenges, from managing stress to maintaining healthy relationships. It's about finding calm in the chaos as well as clarity in the confusion, which often accompanies college experiences. Whether you're a college student or a parent considering buying the book as a gift, this guide is a resource for understanding and implementing mindfulness practices. It's about equipping you with the tools to find peace, balance, and joy in the everyday moments. This journey into the deep is not just about learning; it's about transforming how you experience life, especially during your college years.

Mindfulness isn't just a practice; it's a gateway to a more present, aware, and fulfilling existence. Whether you're dealing with academic pressures, social anxieties, or finding your genuine identity, mindfulness offers a steady way to guide you through the complexities of college life and beyond. Except, maybe you're not doing any of that? Maybe, right now, you're a slacker who takes a bong hit first thing in the morning before classes. Mindfulness is still for you – it makes highs higher, lows more tolerable, and enhances creativity beyond your current baseline. We've written this book to be useful for the person trying to avoid therapy and the person who enjoys therapy. Whether you've already got your sh*t together, or you're a work in progress, mindfulness is a tool and a way of life that can help you level up, or just come to terms with loving yourself. Either way, it's a W.

What Is Mindfulness?

Mindfulness is about being fully present and engaged in the moment, without judgment. It's a skill that can be practiced in many forms, from meditation to simply being aware of your breathing. We follow the well-known mindfulness teacher Jon Kabat-Zinn who describes mindfulness as "paying attention." Mindfulness, he defines more specifically as "an openhearted, moment-to-moment, non-judgmental awareness." Mindfulness boils down to intentionally paying attention. Paying attention includes being aware of the present moment, but also having space in your brain to maintain future events and responsibilities - again, without judgment or anxiety. If someone were to throw a baseball at your face, your awareness would guide you to throw up your hands and protect yourself, right? If you are hiking along the edge of a cliff, your awareness is heightened. These are both moments of "paying attention." There's a baseline of mindfulness that relatively healthy people experience at any given moment. This basic ability to pay attention keeps us safe and allows us to interact with our environment.

Most of us maintain the ability to react in these moments. But how many of us act in these moments, maintaining our power and agency telling the universe that you're here! So often in today's world, especially for young people, things like social media, homework, jobs, and more, cloud our ability to be fully present in whatever the moment is that we're living, diminishing our ability to make a meaningful impact on the world. We're distracted. We're tired. We're constantly on guard - ever oriented in a direction that really matters for ourselves and for maintaining the ability to act and not react.

Mindfulness involves orienting ourselves towards a greater ability to act in and upon the world, rather than react to it. Mindfulness, according to mindful leadership author Kara Coleman, "offers the opportunity to improve the way you decide and direct, the way you engage and lead. It can be the difference between making a hasty decision that creates huge headaches or reaching a thoughtful conclusion that enables success." To put this in terms of the baseball throw, would you be oriented in the present moment enough that you experience the throw with distraction or anxiety, or like Neo from The Matrix, dodging bullets and maintaining your composure? If you're hiking the Grand Canyon, do you have the bandwidth to enjoy the experience, even setting an intention about what you'd like to get out of it, or is the fear of falling overwhelming your ability to be present in the moment? Put in the terms of this book, are you living with depth?

What does it mean for something to be "deep?" Sure, the idea of something being "deep" has become a cliché. We usually associate it with something philosophical, complicated, or hard to understand. Most of the time, when we hear somebody say "That's Deep" these days, they're being sarcastic. Yet, the reference actually means something pointed inward, towards yourself, as in "how deep can you look into yourself." Most of us spend most of our time, day in and day out, at our "surface level," bouncing from one responsibility to another, exhausting our minds and bodies, telling ourselves we are being productive, but never really allowing ourselves to experience why we're doing any of that stuff to begin with. Kabat-Zinn offers more wisdom when he writes about why mindfulness matters: "It is not the content of your experience that is important. What is important is our ability to be aware of that content..." Can you hear the difference? What we mean by "surface level" is when we stay focused on the content of what's going on in our lives – learning that algebraic equation, writing your essay on Henry V, talking to your friend about their recent breakup, etc. All of that content matters in one way or another, but if we are disconnected from the "depth" of our experiences, we'll never be in a position to feel or experience joy, gratitude, or even anger. When we're disoriented from the depth of experience, we're likely to have emotions happen to us from time to time, but rarely would we be in the position to experience and fully process those emotions. Mindfulness is the name we give to what amounts to a choice to dive into the depths of ourselves and our interactions with other people, swimming beneath the surface of what we experience and seeking an experience of connectedness not available on the surface.

What Is Meditation?

Meditation, you've probably heard of. It's when you sit down with your legs crossed, focus on your breathing, and look like an idiot, right? Well, yes and no. Those popular images of people meditating and maybe chanting strange humming sounds is a part of what meditation involves, but it's not the whole picture.

Introduction

Meditation "is really an inward gesture that inclines the heart and mind (seen as one seamless whole) toward a full-spectrum awareness of the present moment just as it is, accepting whatever is happening simply because it is already happening" (Kabat-Zinn). Kabat-Zinn goes on to define meditation as "inner orientation," a kind of "radical acceptance" of all that is. That image of the guy sitting cross-legged leaves us thinking that meditation is a technique used to accomplish something. Really, it is a technique to accomplish nothing. Here's what we mean. Yes, meditation includes doing different things – saying things, sitting quietly, focusing on your breathing, etc. And, you'll learn about several of these techniques across this book. But for us, as for Kabat-Zinn, these techniques "are orienting vehicles pointing at ways of being...in relationship to the present moment and to one's own mind and one's own experience...a way of being appropriate to the circumstances one finds oneself in, in any and every moment." Hence, meditation is a way of accomplishing *no-thing*. Which is exactly what makes it so amazing and effective.

Think of it this way. There are two ways of looking at the world, or two parts of the world to look at, the good and the bad. Suppose all that we do, all that "surface-level" stuff is trying to make the world a better place. That's wonderful, it really is. But do you ever get fully where you are trying to go, with all that "surface-level" stuff? No, of course not. We're not suggesting you stop whatever you're doing. We just want you to dive. When you dive down, you're forced to release all the judgment about the world being good or bad. More importantly, you're forced to release all the judgment about YOU being good or bad. This is what happens when you meditate. You orient yourself to the world as it is. Even if it's only as long as you can hold or take a breath, the world stops being a place you need to fix. The world stops being a place you need to leave a mark on. The world stops being disconnected from you and your will and desire. You become the world – if only for a moment, you become the world. You orient yourself to the world as it is. In doing so, your will, your Self, your Ego, your brain, gets a break. Meditation amounts to a series of techniques that waves and water droplets use to remember that they are the ocean. That's deep.

Another way of understanding depth is offered by Servaas van Beekum, a mindfulness expert, who says that mindfulness is all about conditioning "deeper thinking," and that deeper thinking allows one to be "in contact with oneself and other, with one's own and other's deeper sensations, emotions, drives, thoughts, motivations and shadows." Beekum goes on to offer the clichéd idea of us as an iceberg. Like an iceberg's direction is really determined by the parts of it that we cannot see, humans are the same, and so going deep with mindfulness offers an opportunity to plan for the future because you know who you're dealing with at a deeper level.

Arguably, the need for the depth mindfulness and meditation offers has never been greater. In today's fast-paced world, mindfulness has become more than just a practice — it's a necessity. Its rising popularity reflects our collective need for ways to stay grounded amidst life's challenges. The fact that turning inward is treated with sarcasm so often is a testament to just how far society is from being oriented in a healthy way. Here's a sample of the different ways mindfulness is positively impacting people and the world each and every day:

- Combating Chronic Stress: In a fast-paced, high-pressure society, chronic stress is a widespread issue. Mindfulness practices offer effective tools for managing stress, reducing its long-term impact on mental and physical health.

- Addressing Anxiety and Depression: With rising rates of anxiety and depression, especially among younger populations, mindfulness provides a non-pharmacological approach to mitigate these conditions, promoting mental resilience and emotional stability.

- Counteracting Distraction and Information Overload: In the digital age, where distractions are constant, mindfulness helps in improving focus and concentration. It enables individuals to navigate through information overload more effectively, enhancing productivity and cognitive functioning.

- Alleviating Emotional Reactivity: In a socially and

politically charged environment, mindfulness equips individuals with the ability to regulate emotions. This is crucial for constructive interpersonal interactions and for maintaining mental equilibrium in challenging situations.

- Reducing Feelings of Loneliness and Social Isolation: Mindfulness can foster a sense of connectedness and reduce feelings of loneliness, which are increasingly prevalent in today's society. It encourages a sense of community and belonging.

- Improving Relationships: Mindfulness encourages empathy and active listening, which are key for healthy personal and professional relationships. It helps in resolving conflicts more peacefully and in building stronger, more meaningful connections.

- Enhancing Self-Awareness and Personal Growth: In a world that often emphasizes external success, mindfulness brings the focus back to self-awareness and personal development, encouraging individuals to understand and cultivate their inner selves.

If you're reading this book, and if you've made it this far, you probably already believe that mindfulness is beneficial, and you'd be right! Study after study continues to show that mindfulness is one of the most effective ways to find happiness in life, and physical and mental well-being, too. But you might still be wondering "How" it works. That's what *That's Deep.* is all about, introducing actionable steps and exercises that teach college students how to do all this. Let's start now.

Take a breath.

Now take a slower breath.

Now take a third breath. Try to make it even slower than the last.

If you are anything like us, the first few intentional breaths almost always feel "shaky" on the exhale, like you are on the verge of tears. That's what we call a "release." That *IS* the emotions that come with crying or with emotional fits. The difference is you're releasing them now, with your breath, rather than waiting for a crisis. Merely breathing allows for the physiological release of emotions. This promotes the production of oxytocin in the brain. You immediately feel better, chemically. All from paying attention to your breathing. Not even that. All from paying attention to a single breath.

Take another breath.

And another one…

You are meditating. In your breath, your single breath, you are interfacing with all that is. There really is no distinction between you and the rest of the world or the universe if you're looking closely enough at your breath. This is the moment of orientation. It doesn't have to be twenty minutes, in fact, it's almost never twenty minutes. This is where we want to orient you now – to your breath. To a single breath. All of the benefits of meditation are happening to you in a single breath. The only catch is that you have to do it on purpose. You have to be intentional about making the magic happen. So don't just file this away in your above average IQ brain and think that you're going to be meditating all the time because you're breathing all the time. It doesn't work that way. Meditation is not a euphemism for laziness. You can't do it on autopilot. You have to do it. Which means, ironically, meditation is when you do nothing.

Orienting Yourself to the Book

That's Deep: A Mindfulness Guide for College Students embarks on a transformative journey into the practice of mindfulness, tailored specifically for the college experience. We wrote this book because the book we wanted – a guide for mindfulness not written by a shrink or a parent or some self-righteous guru – didn't really exist. So, we wrote a college guide for mindfulness written by college students. It's been important for us to write something that we'd actually use.

Introduction

You might be wondering who "we" are, who is Lule West?

We're a group of college students from Lehigh University in Bethlehem, Pennsylvania, who participated in a program called Lehigh Launch where we spent a semester in the American west. This semester combines the essence of a study-abroad program with experiential, place-based learning, and leadership designed to challenge and empower students both on and off campus. The ten of us first came together in August of 2023 beginning our adventure with a three-week National Outdoor Leadership School (NOLS) backpacking expedition in Wyoming. This kick-started our semester where we took a full course load of classes and integrated the information into usable knowledge.

Our travels took us through stunning locations like the Absaroka Mountains in Wyoming and Sinks Canyon State Park. We ventured through urban centers like Denver and Golden, Colorado, where we engaged with locals and visited science and manufacturing labs. In Leadville, Colorado, we learned about local politics, speaking with a County Commissioner against the backdrop of the Rocky Mountains. The curriculum was diverse, covering subjects like the History of the American West, Conservation Biology, Shamanism, and Western Literature. We also tackled contemporary issues such as water management in Engineering, local governance in Politics and Identity, and regional challenges in Policy Challenges. These classes weren't confined to the classroom; they were alive with hands-on experiences and real-world applications. After all, the program motto is: "Because life isn't divided into majors. And not all classrooms have walls." Our journey concluded in Santa Fe, New Mexico, where we dove into the complex histories of Native Americans and Hispanics.

One of the classes we took during the semester was on mindfulness. We learned about the history of mindfulness and its rising popularity, as well as many different mindfulness techniques such as meditation - which we've included here. Yet, we were frustrated that there didn't seem to be a book specifically for college students that covered the who, what, where, why, and how of mindfulness. There are thousands of mindfulness guides and handbooks these days, and college and university campuses have more people practicing mindfulness than ever. But a book just didn't exist that put all the important info into a usable package. The book we quote from often in this guide is Jon Kabat-Zinn's *Coming to Our Senses*, which is over five-hundred pages!

Ain't Nobody Got Time for That!

So, we decided, along with our professor, to write the book we wish would have existed for our class. Our grade no longer depended on exams or research papers - whether we made an A or not would be decided by whether we wrote a book worth your time. Now, after way more work than a midterm or final would have required, we present to you *That's Deep. A Mindfulness Guide for College Students.*

We've organized the book to be as reader-friendly as possible, a kind of manual or bathroom book with some depth. Take a second to thumb through the book, and you'll notice that we have put the exercises in shadowboxes to make them easy to find. We have also recorded each exercise in an audio format available by following this QR Code:

That's Deep.
Audio
Exercises

The QR code will take you directly to the audio files that go with each chapter exercise. We want to mention, if you choose to read the practice and not listen to the audio, make sure you complete each step slowly. Take your time. Pause between each individual direction, do not just read it through like you would a novel. We've also included a "Common Challenges" section at the end of the book for the moments where your mindfulness journey gets tough. And, we've offered Reflection Questions for all you overachievers, and tried to offer lots of usable lists and bullet points in the chapters. As busy college students, we need hard and fast actionable info, so we've implemented that into this book. In the event you find yourself on a third paragraph with no end in sight, take a breath. We've worked hard to make sure you never have to read more than three pages in one sitting. Seriously, we've written the book we have wanted, if we ever would have imagined writing a book on mindfulness for college students. Now that we've written it, it's become our guide for keeping our sanity across this amazing time called "college."

From the very outset in "Who Are You?," the guide dives deep into the heart of identity, exploring the nuanced interplay between mindfulness and the multifaceted aspects of the self. Through personal stories and exercises like Progressive Muscle Relaxation, this first chapter aims to foster an inclusive environment where all students, regardless of background or creed, can engage with mindfulness to confront societal 'isms' and embrace their unique college journey, especially the often-overlooked First Generation students. The common goal for all of us is to graduate and continue to accomplish our goals, though that burden can potentially be weighing you down.

In Chapter Two, "C's Make Degrees," speaks to the pressures of academic performance, offering solace and practical strategies to those grappling with the fear of failure. Through Alyssa's narrative, readers learn how mindfulness can be a tool for building self-confidence and establishing effective coping mechanisms. The Quieting the Mind Meditation serves as a touchstone exercise for returning to the present and breaking free from the binds of academic anxiety. The pile of paperwork that seems to never stop, can potentially lead to burn out, which is where self-care can come into play.

Self-care is not merely an indulgence but rather a necessity, as outlined in Chapter Three, "Treat Yo'Self." This section dispels myths about self-care, urging a balance between work and play, and highlighting the critical role of positive sleep schedules. Amaris's Story, paired with The Body-Scan Meditation, provides practical insights into how a mindful approach can significantly uplift mental and physical health. Another aspect that can affect your mental health due to various factors can be the world of social media.

In Chapter Four, "IYKYK," captures the culture of modern college life, addressing the complex worlds of social media, peer pressure, body image, and partying. The personal accounts and exercises, including an exercise of Affirmations for Social Confidence, act as a compass to steer through the often tumultuous waters of social life, advocating for mindful presence as a tool for self-empowerment. Within the whirlwind of social media, you can find yourself in a new friend group or with a new partner.

The intricacies of personal relationships are at the heart of Chapter Five, "Situationships." Sofia's Story opens the dialogue about the shifts in dynamics with family, friends, and romantic interests that college life brings. The Lovingkindness Meditation provides a practice for nurturing compassion, not only for others but also for oneself. You can stretch your compassion through a colorful exploration of belief and tradition.

Chapter Six, "What's Your Zodiac?," invites a broader conversation about religion, spirituality, and the rise of alternative practices like astrology, crystals, and aromatherapy. Maria's Story and the Walking Meditation extend an invitation to contemplate one's place within the universe.

Finally, Chapter Seven is all about "Levelin' Up" and directs your gaze forward, beyond the confines of college life. It equips students with the mindfulness tools necessary for building resilience, embracing self-care, and leading a mindful life long after graduation. Here, the stories and exercises, such as the Lying Down Meditation, serve as both culmination and commencement of a lifelong mindfulness journey.

Chapter One

Who Are You?

Mindfulness & You

College is a place of transformation. That's the first rule they don't teach you in any orientation. The friends you used to share secrets with, the routines you meticulously maintained, the place you called home - they all go through a whirlwind transformation the moment you step onto a college campus. Suddenly, you're navigating uncharted waters, both academically and socially. New faces and voices fill your world, challenging your thoughts and beliefs with every lecture, discussion, and late-night dorm-room chat. But amidst the chaos of this new chapter in your life, one thing remains unchanged - you.

Those core aspects of yourself, the things you know, the beliefs you hold dear, the talents you've honed, and the values you cherish - they are still there. Sure, college can and should influence them, expand your horizons, and inform your worldview. It's part of what makes this journey so transformative. However, just because your surroundings have shifted so abruptly doesn't mean that who you are should change, especially not as quickly as your world.

This new journey can feel overwhelming. The pressure to fit in, to be seen as "normal," and to blend in with the crowd can all be daunting. But let us tell you something we wish we'd known when we started this adventure - you don't have to sacrifice your identity to find your place in college. In fact, mindfulness offers an opportunity to stay checked in with who you've been, negotiate the opportunities for transforming who you are, all while retaining or developing a powerful sense of identity. Are you ready?

In this first chapter, we're going to explore the complex world of identity formation. We'll discuss the importance of inclusivity, not just as a buzzword, but as a guiding principle. We'll discuss what it means to be a first-generation student and the unique challenges and triumphs that come with that distinction. We'll navigate the path to finding your voice, and learn that your identity can be your greatest strength.

This chapter is your compass, your companion, and your reminder that you don't have to leave your true self behind to thrive in this brand new world. In the pages that follow, we invite you to embrace your identity, champion inclusivity, and celebrate the incredible journey of being a college student. Whether you're the tenth generation of your family to make it to college, or a first-generation student struggling with whether or not you belong at your university, this book is for you.

Welcome to the adventure. You're not alone, and your identity is your superpower. Let's begin on this transformative journey together, and in the end, you'll see that things change during college, but not everything about you has to change.

To navigate this transformative period, we'd like to introduce the idea of mindfulness. As we show across this guide, mindfulness is a powerful tool to help you stay connected with your true self in a journey full of change. Jon Kabat-Zinn is the father of a science-based system called Mindfulness Based Stress Reduction (MBSR). His system has gained popularity over the last thirty years and he's gained the reputation of the go-to guy for all-things mindfulness in the western world. He defines mindfulness as "openhearted, moment-to-moment, non-judgmental awareness." During your time in college, you have the freedom and opportunity to go deep into self-discovery, discovering your authentic self or if you even resonate with the idea of "authenticity." In the words of Jon Kabat-Zinn, he advises that, "It does help if I remind myself to ask my heart from time to time what is most important right now, in this moment, and listen very carefully for the response." This is what mindfulness promises. And, you can achieve it as much with meditation or by simply sitting down to read a book like this one. Let's start there.

Take a moment now to center yourself in the present moment. Find a quiet place to sit or lie down, and focus on your breath. Inhale deeply, feeling the air fill your lungs, and exhale slowly, releasing any tension or stress stored in your body. As you continue reading, keep paying attention to your breath and what's happening around you in the current moment. You don't need to be "good" at it, or even know what you're doing. Just pause for a moment, take a deep breath, and bring your attention to the moment as it's unfolding around you.

Take one more breath. Feels good, right?

Obviously, we don't know who you are. But we know that who you are matters to you. It matters to us. In this moment, as you read, you are completely "you." Take confidence in knowing yourself right now – in this moment. Self-awareness is empowering, and it cultivates confidence and peace of mind. When you embrace who you are, you project an image of sincerity and self-confidence. This self-assuredness can empower you to navigate the challenges and opportunities of college life with poise and authenticity. Confidence in your identity translates to confidence in your decisions and actions. This moment of mindfulness is a reminder that embracing your genuine identity allows you to express your thoughts, emotions, and values honestly and openly. This is essential for maintaining good mental health during your college years. Incorporating mindfulness throughout your college journey can be a powerful tool to manage stress and enhance your over-all well-being. This technique helps you reconnect with your true self and align with your passions and values. The act of mindfulness serves as a beacon of self-ac-ceptance, drawing like-minded individuals and real connections into your life. When you stay true to your-self, you naturally attract friends, mentors, and allies who appreciate and respect you for who you are.

This alignment with your "realest" self has the poten-tial to ignite your passions and provide you with a clear sense of purpose, which can drive your academic and personal pursuits with unwavering enthusiasm. College life can be demanding, with its share of academic, per-sonal, and social challenges. Your identity equips you with the resilience and adaptability needed to navigate these hurdles. By remaining true to who you are, you develop a strong sense of self, enabling you to face adversity with grace and bounce back from setbacks with renewed strength. Being grounded in your identi-ty encourages inclusivity and diversity within your col-lege community; you set a powerful example for others to be themselves and accept others, too. This sets the stage for an inclusive and diverse environment where everyone feels encouraged to express their unique identities without fear of judgment or discrimination. Your authenticity can foster a culture of acceptance, understanding, and mutual respect.

College is a profound period in your life when you're given the freedom and opportunity to dive deep into self-discovery. It's a moment of your life where you en-counter the kaleidoscope of different ways that people live their lives, discovering people from diverse back-grounds, cultures, and life experiences, who all bring a colorful mix of viewpoints and stories to discover. This variety is the counterpoint to your authentic iden-tity. We don't mean it is the opposite of it – we mean that the things you experience in college that are new or different, or that even cause a bit of defensive dis-comfort, are the other side of the coin that is "you." We're not just feeding you some weird propaganda or fake news. This is legit, and goes back to ancient wisdom: Who "you" are is always made up of all the other "you's" you come in contact with. Amazingly, one of the most mindful ways of getting to know yourself in college involves getting to know other people and practicing "leaning in" to moments of uncertainty. So, here are some tips on how to do that:

Embrace Introspection: Your journal becomes your map of self-discovery, a compass for navigating your inner world. Reflect on your values, dreams, beliefs, and past experiences. Discover what excites you and what you hold dear. Through introspection, you'll gain insights into your authentic self.

- Join Clubs or Communities Outside Your Knowledge or Comfort-Zone: College provides a wide variety of different experiences. Step out of your comfort zone, explore topics beyond your major, and engage in extracurricular activities. Hey, you might be a choir kid and not even know it yet! Uncharted territories may often hold the treasures of your true passions and strengths, so embrace new experiences with an open mind.

- Seek Guidance: Some professors are gems, and they can be your compass in navigating new territory. Unfortunately, others may not be, so it's important to find those people who resonate with you. Don't hesitate to ask for their wisdom or help; their insights can help you unlock your interests and talents.

- Embrace Failure as a Stepping Stone: Failure and setbacks are part of your journey, it is what makes us grow. Accept these circumstances as teachers, not enemies, guiding you along the path to self-discovery and personal growth. Rise above them with grace and resilience, gaining insights into your true form along the way.

- Connect with Like-Minded People: Your peers are fellow travelers on the path of self-discovery. Connect with those who share your passions and values. Friendships born of shared interests strengthen your identity and offer companionship on your quest.

- Embrace and Celebrate Your Uniqueness: Don't stay focused on what sets you apart, everyone's path looks different. What sets you apart is your strength. Embrace your quirks, cultural background, passions, and challenges. Celebrate your individuality, for it's the masterpiece that uniquely makes you, you!

- Keep an Open Mind: Self-discovery is a dynamic, ever-evolving process. Be open to new experiences, changing perspectives, and the personal growth that accompanies them. Your identity is not fixed; it's a beautiful, transformative journey.

College really marks the beginning of your quest for self-discovery, and the lessons you learn will illuminate your path. It's a transformative time of self-reflection, diverse experiences, the wisdom of mentors, and the lessons of failures. In many ways, college is the start of your unique journey into adulthood, and it all begins with the deep, lingering, eternal question, "Who am I?" Notice we're emphasizing that this is the beginning of the journey, not the end. It's okay to not know who you are by the time you graduate. Mindfulness and meditation are not about creating yourself, but coming to love and accept yourself wherever and whoever you are. Mindfulness helps with self-discovery throughout your life, so it's okay to take your time and relax into the experience. Embrace this journey, and allow mindfulness to be your guide.

The Benefits of Mindfulness for Identity

Embracing the journey of self-discovery in college while incorporating mindfulness practices can profoundly impact your personal, academic, and professional life. Mindfulness allows you to connect with your authentic self on a deeper level, providing numerous benefits throughout your college years and beyond. Mindfulness, as Jon Kabat-Zinn beautifully puts it, means "paying attention in a particular way; on purpose, in the present moment, and nonjudgmentally." Let's focus on how mindfulness further amplifies the advantages of finding your true identity during your college journey:

- Self-Confidence and Self-Esteem: Mindfulness encourages self-awareness by helping you recognize your thoughts and emotions without judgment. Through this practice, you can observe self-doubts and insecurities and learn to let them go. This newfound non-judgemental self-awareness can translate into a boost in self-confidence and self-esteem. As you grow more in tune with your authentic self, you begin to see yourself in a more positive light, which fosters greater self-confidence in making choices, engaging in social interactions, and pursuing your academic and career goals.

- Enhanced Decision-Making: Mindfulness allows you to focus on the present moment, reducing stress and anxiety about the future. This clarity empowers you to make more deliberate and aligned choices. By having a deeper understanding of your values and priorities, you can make decisions that align with your personal goals and aspirations, minimizing the stress and uncertainty often associated with major life choices.

- Improved Mental Health: Practicing mindfulness during college can significantly impact your mental well-being. By observing your thoughts and emotions without judgment, you become better equipped to manage stress, anxiety, and other emotional challenges. This understanding of your true self empowers you to make choices that prioritize your mental health, resulting in a happier and healthier college experience. Jon Kabat-Zinn's words, "You can't stop the waves, but you can learn to surf," remind us that mindfulness equips us to ride the waves of life.

- Strengthened Relationships: Mindfulness fosters empathy and emotional intelligence by promoting self-awareness. When you know yourself better, you can relate more genuinely to others. Authentic connections with like-minded individuals become more accessible, leading to deeper and more meaningful relationships. You'll find yourself surrounded by friends and mentors who appreciate you for who you truly are, creating a strong support network that is invaluable during your college journey.

- Academic Excellence: Mindfulness enhances your ability to focus on the present moment, allowing you to engage more deeply with your studies. When you're engaged in subjects and activities that genuinely interest you, your motivation and enthusiasm for learning soar. This passion can lead to higher grades, more meaningful academic projects, and a greater sense of fulfillment in your studies.

- Professional Success: The self-awareness and self-confidence gained from mindfulness extend into your professional life. As you develop a deeper understanding of your strengths and values, you can make more informed career choices. This will lead to a career that aligns with your true passions, resulting in greater job satisfaction and success in the long run.

- Resilience and Adaptability: In college, you'll face various challenges, from academic pressures to personal setbacks. Mindfulness equips you with the resilience and adaptability needed to navigate these challenges gracefully. By being aware of your true self, you'll be more capable of handling adversity and bouncing back from setbacks with renewed strength.

- A Fulfilling Life: Ultimately, the practice of mindfulness leads to a more fulfilling life. It helps you appreciate the present moment, making challenges easier to bear. Regardless of life's ups and downs, mindfulness offers a sense of fulfillment that can be a driving force for well-being and excellence in all aspects of your life.

- Contribution to Society: Mindfulness not only benefits you but also equips you to make a positive impact on society. By knowing yourself, your values, and your passions, you can channel your energy and talents toward causes that matter to you, becoming a catalyst for positive change in your community and the world at large.

- Personal Growth and Continuous Learning: Self-discovery is a lifelong journey, and college is just the beginning. As you grow and evolve, you'll continue to learn more about yourself and the world around you. Embracing this process of self-discovery with mindfulness can lead to a life filled with personal growth, curiosity, and a deep appreciation for the journey of self-improvement.

In conclusion, navigating college is not just a personal endeavor; it's a transformative and invaluable experience that can shape your entire life. The practice of mindfulness amplifies the benefits of self-discovery, enhancing your personal development, emotional well-being, academic and professional success, fulfilling relationships, and your contribution to society. It's a journey that ultimately leads to a life lived in harmony with your true self, resulting in lasting happiness, purpose, and success. So embrace the journey. You're on the path to unlocking a future that's uniquely yours. As Jon Kabat-Zinn has written, "Wherever you go, there you are."

Inclusivity and Diversity

Picture this: a vibrant campus where diversity is a superpower, a place where various cultures, backgrounds, and experiences come together to create magic. As the previous section emphasizes, these different people and experiences are effectively the other side of "you." That's what we're striving for – an inclusive and diverse college environment that's not just essential, but incredibly exciting because it is how you are challenged, emboldened, enlivened, and empowered. This goes for people no matter their political affiliation or priorities. Can you imagine a college experience where a young person is not passionate about the issues that mark us as a society? We can't and we don't want to either. Embracing inclusiveness and diversity is not about political correctness; it's about tapping into the resources offered by different perspectives, ideas, and talents.

What does it mean to be inclusive? Inclusivity refers to the practice of ensuring that individuals or groups feel welcomed, respected, and valued within a community or environment. It's about creating spaces and opportunities where differences are acknowledged and celebrated, enabling everyone to participate fully. For example, in a classroom, inclusivity might involve providing resources in multiple languages to accommodate non-native speakers. Outside the classroom, it could mean making sure that people with different physical abilities feel welcome at a party.

Okay, so what about diversity? Diversity refers to the presence of differences within a given setting, encompassing aspects such as race, gender, age, ethnicity, religion, sexual orientation, and socio-economic status. It's about recognizing and appreciating these unique characteristics and perspectives that individuals bring to a group or community. For instance, a class might include students from different cultural backgrounds, offering varied viewpoints. On campus, diversity can be reflected in a student body that represents multiple nationalities. In literature, diversity may be seen in stories that feature characters with a wide range of experiences and identities.

Here's a secret – the push for inclusiveness and diversity on campus is not simply a matter of doing right by the little guy or marginalized folks. Compassion is a piece of the puzzle, but it's also about getting the highest number of different ideas and experiences into a seminar room together and battling it out to fit the ideas together or determine which idea is the most sensible. And all these different ideas are created from the different experiences that we have as individuals. Colleges try to make good use of our differences. That's one reason you see so many TikTok videos of people going on rants on college campuses. Yes, sometimes they get out of hand, but these things are supposed to happen at college. That's the point. Think of it as building a toolbox stocked with the best tools from around the world. Beyond academics, inclusivity and diversity does try to create a welcoming atmosphere that's like a home away from home. But it's not just about feeling warm and fuzzy – it's a necessity. Discrimination and exclusion can cast a shadow over your college experience and impact your well-being. For those who are excluded or who are coming from historically-marginalized communities, feeling left out hurts. And even for those coming from historically-dominant communities, exclusion means their ideas aren't being tested to ensure they're good ones. When we create an inclusive environment, it's a win for everyone.

One powerful strategy for both prioritizing inclusivity and diversity as well as for making the task of it easier is mindfulness. Here are some ways mindfulness can manifest a more inclusive college environment for you and everyone on your campus:

- Self-Awareness: Mindfulness encourages self-reflection and awareness. It helps individuals recognize their biases and prejudices, enabling them to work on overcoming them. When we are mindful, we become more open to seeing our own shortcomings and growth opportunities in terms of inclusivity and diversity.

- Empathy and Compassion: Mindfulness cultivates empathy and compassion. By practicing non-judgmental awareness, we become more attuned to the experiences and feelings of others. This heightened empathy can lead to greater understanding and support for those from diverse backgrounds.

- Conflict Resolution: In diverse settings, conflicts may arise due to differing perspectives. Mindfulness equips individuals with better tools for handling these conflicts and disagreements. It promotes patience, understanding, and a willingness to find common ground.

- Reducing Stereotyping: Mindfulness can reduce automatic stereotyping and judgment. When we are mindful, we become more conscious of our thought patterns and can challenge stereotypes or biases as they arise.

- Inclusive Decision-Making: In mindful organizations and educational institutions, decision-making processes are often more inclusive. Leaders and decision-makers are more likely to consider the other perspectives and needs of a diverse group of stakeholders.

Incorporating mindfulness into your daily routine can be as simple as setting aside a few minutes each day for meditation or practicing mindful breathing. As college students, embracing mindfulness can lead to a more inclusive and diverse academic experience that will equip us with valuable skills for the future. At the end of the chapter, we will have a mindfulness exercise called Progressive Muscle Relaxation, which is a deep relaxation technique that has been shown to effectively control stress and anxiety. Inclusivity and diversity are not just buzzwords; they are the heart of a better college experience. Inclusivity is our mission. When we embrace the strength in our differences, we become part of something extraordinary. By being aware, empathetic, and committed to change, we can shape the culture of our campus and empower those who have experienced discrimination. As college students, we are the agents of change, and our journey doesn't stop when we graduate. It continues as we carry these values into the broader world. That's what college is all about, isn't it?

Confronting the 'Isms

Now let's talk about a topic that's essential, but often uncomfortable: the 'isms.' You know, racism, sexism, ageism, and all those exclusions we noted above that can make our college experience more challenging. Here's the deal – it's not all doom and gloom. We have the power to confront and change the narrative, and mindfulness can be a helpful tool in this journey.

So, why should we even care about these 'Isms'? Well, they're like invisible barriers that can hold us back, potentially leaving us wondering if we deserve to be in this college. Being discriminated against based on our identities can create a sense of exclusion, making us question our self-worth, impacting our mental health. But when we stand up against the 'isms,' we're not just changing things for a few, we're changing things for all of us. The change that happens will create a college environment where everyone has a fair shot at success.

Now, how can mindfulness help us take on these invisible monsters that keep on pestering us? It starts with self-awareness and emotional intelligence. Mindfulness is the practice of being present in the moment, accepting our thoughts and feelings without judgment. By practicing mindfulness, we become more attuned to our own biases, preconceived notions, and reactions to others. This works for the victim of racism as much as the so-called "racist." Say you're a person of color who's experiencing racism from a classmate or even a professor. Though it can be challenging to reach out, there are certain steps you should take in addressing it, such as going to your Student Services office, talking to friends and sharing experiences, or even filing a formal complaint. But self-care is also essential. Mindfulness is not a cure for racism, not at all, but it offers an opportunity for taking care of yourself amidst it. Mindful breathing practices, sitting to meditate, or walking through a park, are all opportunities to rest, check in with yourself, and process emotions in order to make sure that you're acting to improve your well-being rather than just reacting passively to the situation. Do not be afraid to utilize the resources available to you, whether it is reaching out to your educational professionals, choosing mindfulness, or both.

If you're the racist in someone else's story, even if you might not think that about yourself, there are ways that mindfulness can have a positive impact on that story. Well, if you're some outright white supremacist, you can go f*ck yourself and throw away this book, you won't listen to us anyway. But, if you're one of the countless folks whose racism is unconscious or unrecognized, and will listen, here are some tips. The first step to making change happen is recognition. Mindfulness practices can help you to be more aware and thoughtful before you speak, as well as be more sensitive to those around you and to yourself. Finally, mindfulness can also help to open your ears and heart to listening and accepting constructive feedback from others.

There's a common self-help adage: hurting people are the ones who hurt people. Here's where mindfulness can help. Imagine how much more bandwidth that a**hole professor or student would have to be present and fair with all of the students if they would take the time to meditate for fifteen minutes. Most often, people are mean to other people when something's going wrong for them, that's usually totally disconnected from the person they're mean to, or even oppressing. Importantly, it isn't the responsibility of the victim of racism to bring a**holes along on their healing journey and mindfulness isn't the only thing needed for confronting the 'isms. Laws, economics, and other "macro" or "structural" changes often need to be made, too. But mindfulness is what this book's about and we think it has something to offer for the 'Isms. Jon Kabat-Zinn once wrote "Just by meditating, by sitting down and being still, you can change yourself and the world. In fact, just by sitting down and being still, in a small but not insignificant way, you already have." Whether you've been a victim of the 'Isms, taken your identity as an ally in the fight against these 'Isms, or even been the a**hole, meditating has the ability to fundamentally impact your sense of self and your well-being for the better.

Mindfulness helps us address stereotypes and biases when we encounter them. Imagine this: you're in a class discussion, and someone makes a comment that reinforces a stereotype. Mindfulness can help you pause, reflect on your response, and choose to educate others with empathy and compassion, changing the story right there and then. Expanding your horizons and realizing that the world is a lot more diverse and complex than you thought is a major part of the college experience.

Mindfulness can assist you in approaching each person with an open mind and leaving your assumptions about who they are at the door.

College might seem like a great equalizer, but mindfulness can help you recognize the unique experiences and backgrounds of your fellow students. And, let's not forget creating safe spaces. Mindfulness can help you be fully present and engaged in these spaces, where you can share your experiences, seek advice, and find support without judgment.

Confronting the 'Isms isn't a one-time battle; it's an ongoing journey. We can and should make our campuses a place where everyone feels valued, respected, and empowered. It's not just about transforming our college experience; it's about creating ripples of change that extend into society. We are the generation that can make this happen, and that's something extraordinary.

First Generation Students

Picture your first day on a college campus – the mix of excitement and nervousness, the big dreams and the looming challenges. It's a day filled with possibilities and a dash of uncertainty. For many students, it's a rite of passage, almost like following a well-worn path, guided by the wisdom of family and friends who've been there before. But what if you're a first-generation college student? Your journey is a lot different - where you're the first one to embark on the path, the one to walk through the woods without any guidance. You're like a pioneer, venturing into unknown territory, armed with determination and ambition.

Being a first-generation college student means you're the first in your family to embark on the adventure of higher education. It's a significant milestone to be proud of, but it comes with its challenges. You're like a trailblazer, forging your path through the academic wilderness, and it can be overwhelming and confusing. There's no family playbook to consult when you're juggling finances, choosing classes, and balancing extracurricular activities. The persistent feeling of imposter syndrome - that sense that you don't belong where you are, that you're 'faking it', and the fear that others will find you out - can be like a pesky mosquito buzzing in your ear, making you question your place in this new world. Whether you're a first-gen student or not, understanding this experience is important because it shines a light on the remarkable achievement and unique struggles faced by those who are breaking new ground in higher education. So don't be afraid to come face to face with something new, challenging, and different while you are at college. Yes, you may not have all the same resources accessible to you like your classmates and friends, but don't view that as another obstacle tearing you down, but instead, as a characteristic that makes you more resilient.

Unique Challenges: Overcoming the Odds

As a first-generation college student, you navigate a unique set of challenges:

- Navigating the Unknown: You step into unfamiliar territory without the benefit of family guidance. It's like embarking on a journey without a map, and it can feel daunting. It can leave you feeling disconnected from folks on campus as much as from family and friends back home.

- Financial Struggles: Many first-gen students face significant financial pressures, often requiring part-time jobs to cover tuition or having to support their families. Some college students are juggling more than college, just so that they can be in college.

- Imposter Syndrome: The fear of not belonging in the academic environment is common and can undermine your self-confidence. It is hard to succeed when fear and anxiety of failure take all your energy.

- Balancing Responsibilities: Managing academic commitments alongside work, family obligations, or community involvement can be overwhelming.

- Social and Cultural Adjustments: Adapting to a new social and cultural environment can be a significant challenge, especially when it involves different norms and expectations.

- Academic Pressure: The pressure to excel academically can be intense, as the dreams and hopes of your family often ride on your success, leading to stress and anxiety.

Mindfulness as a Solution

Mindfulness is your anchor in these turbulent waters. It's about being present in the moment, paying attention to your thoughts and feelings without any criticism. Here's how it can help first-gen students:

- Eases Stress: Mindfulness techniques, like deep breathing and meditation, can help reduce stress and anxiety, allowing you to focus on your studies without feeling as overwhelmed. Stress is a part of life; it won't go away. But mindfulness helps to ease the stress so you have more time and energy for yourself.

- Fosters Resilience: It encourages resilience, vital for facing unique challenges, helping you bounce back from setbacks and build confidence in your abilities. Mindfulness offers an opportunity to bounce-back faster from feeling depleted and regular practice increases the amount a person can endure before feeling depleted, too.

- Enhances Focus: Staying focused in college and on future goals, especially while managing multiple responsibilities, becomes easier with mindfulness by improving your concentration. Mindfulness is a kind of rest for your brain and body, helping both to feel "sharper" when it's time to focus.

- Builds Self-Awareness: By practicing mindfulness, you become more in tune with your thoughts and emotions, helping you address imposter syndrome and other negative thought patterns. You see clearly that you do belong right where you are, and that knowledge empowers you to make your mark!

By integrating mindfulness into your first-gen journey, you can build the resilience and inner strength to overcome the unique challenges that come with being a first-generation student. It's a tool that empowers you to embrace the unknown, manage financial stresses, combat imposter syndrome, balance responsibilities, adapt to new environments, and excel academically, all while staying grounded in the present moment.

The first-gen college experience is a remarkable achievement, a journey filled with unique challenges and opportunities. At the end of the day, don't forget to give yourself a pat on the back for all you continue to accomplish. Mindfulness serves as a compass, guiding you through the uncertain terrain, empowering you to thrive in the face of adversity. Remember, it's not just your journey; it's a story worth sharing, understanding, and supporting, for together, we can help first-gen students on their path towards a brighter future.

Jessica's Story

Come along for Jessica's ride through her freshman year. When we first set foot on campus, it was buzzing with activity, right? But for Jessica, things got real confusing real fast. She felt lost, and honestly, kinda anxious, trying to figure out where she fit in this whole new world. I mean, who can blame her? Like, we're all in the same boat, right? College is a total mystery, especially when you're fresh out of high school. Getting used to the college scene is already a big deal, but then there's the whole process of making new friends after four years and deciding what the heck you want to study, and that just adds a heap of stress to the mix.

This forced Jessica to take action and embark on a journey of self-discovery. She decided to participate in various extracurricular activities to find a niche that resonated with her. Her first stop was at her university's drama club. While there, Jessica auditioned for a big part in a play, and she discovered a passion for theater that she never knew she had. The thrill of her performance and the camaraderie with her fellow actors sparked self-actualization.

Encouraged by this new interest, Jessica continued to explore other areas. She joined a volunteer group that works with the community and provides meals to those in need. In this group, she discovered a deep sense of fulfillment and a desire to give something back to the community.

In addition to extracurricular activities, Jessica made a point to take classes that went beyond her major, choosing course topics that sparked her curiosity as often as possible. She took psychology courses, attended philosophy lectures, and even dabbled in art. In these courses, Jessica learned about the depths of the human mind, the philosophical questions that preoccupied great thinkers, and the creativity inherent in them.

Jessica's horizons continued to expand through her interactions with peers. She made friends with people from different backgrounds and had meaningful conversations that challenged her beliefs and broadened her horizons. Jessica tried to see every interaction as an opportunity for self-discovery and personal growth.

As the years progressed, Jessica discovered a love for psychology, coupled with her passion for theater and her desire to positively impact the community. She decided to major in Psychology and minor in Theater, and joined a student-run mental health awareness group so she could use her acting skills to get an important message across.

Through extracurricular activities, courses, and social interactions, Jessica found her true calling. College became a place of self-discovery, and she learned that embracing her passions, values, and unique qualities was the key to discovering her true self.

At each stage of this journey of self-discovery, Jessica felt more connected to her true identity and better prepared to navigate the complexities of college life. She understood that her diverse experiences shaped her into a confident, self-assured, and authentic person.

Ultimately, Jessica's college experience is a testament to the transformative power of self-discovery, where the journey of self-discovery is an ongoing and rewarding process marked by extracurricular activities, coursework, and meaningful social interactions.

Exercise: Progressive Muscle Relaxation

Amid the lively hustle and bustle of college life, the company of stressors and intense emotions often become an unwelcome daily reality for students. It's in these very moments that mindfulness practices prove to be indispensable tools, offering a guiding light through the new sea of college experiences and expectations. This section is here to introduce you to a practice called Progressive Muscle Relaxation, a soothing mindfulness exercise with a clear purpose: to provide relaxation, ease the burden of stress, and nurture a stronger connection between your body and mind, all in the context of your identity formation.

Progressive Muscle Relaxation, or PMR for short, is both uncomplicated and immensely impactful. The process entails a deliberate sequence of tensing and then releasing different muscle groups throughout your body. This journey begins with your toes and gradually ascends to the crown of your head. As you engage in this practice, the rewards are clear. First and foremost, you'll experience a tangible sense of physical relaxation. Then, tensions that may have settled in your muscles begin to dissipate, and the weight of stress feels lighter.

Yet, PMR goes beyond mere physical relief. It's a journey that dives deep into the connection between your body and mind. Through PMR, you begin to understand the subtle cues that your body provides. It's as if you're learning a new language, where the vocabulary consists of the physical manifestations of your emotions and stress. You'll become proficient in interpreting these cues, and this newfound self-awareness will serve as your guiding compass through the sometimes chaotic waters of college life.

Step 1: Find a Quiet Space

Locate a comfortable and quiet place where you can sit or lie down without any disturbances.

Step 2: Begin with Breathing

Take a few deep breaths to center yourself. Inhale slowly through your nose, hold it for a few seconds, and exhale gently through your mouth.

Step 3: Start with Your Toes

As you continue to breathe, focus your attention on your toes. Slowly curl them into a tight ball, holding this tension for a few seconds, and then release. As you do this, be aware of the sensations in your toes.

Step 4: Work Your Way Up Your Body

Continue this process, moving up your body from your feet to your calves, then to your thighs, your stomach, and so on.

- Thighs and Calves: Flex your thigh muscles by straightening your legs and pointing your toes upward. Hold for 5-10 seconds and then relax. Do the same for your calf muscles. Circle back to concentrating on your breath.

- Abdomen: Tense your abdominal muscles by pulling your belly button toward your spine. Hold for 5-10 seconds and then release. Circle back to concentrating on your breath.

- Chest and Back: Tighten your torso by taking a deep breath and holding it for 5-10 seconds. Exhale and let go, feeling the relaxation in your chest and back. Circle back to concentrating on your breath.

- Shoulders and Neck: Raise your shoulders toward your ears, creating tension in your neck and shoulders. Hold for 5-10 seconds, then release, allowing your shoulders to drop as the tension dissipates. Circle back to concentrating on your breath.

- Head: Bring your attention fully to the physical aspect of your head. Move across your head's circumference, checking for any physical sensations such as pain, warmth, tingling, and more. Circle back to concentrating on your breath.

Step 5: Full Body Check

Take a moment to scan your body from head to toe. If you notice any residual tension in specific areas, tense and release those muscles to ensure complete relaxation. As you experience the overall relaxation in your body, allow your mind to release stress and tension. As you progress through this exercise, observe the emotions and sensations that arise. Focus on the sensation of relaxation and peace.

Step 6: Refocus On Your Breath

Always come back to your breath if your mind wanders. Concentrate on your inhales and exhales, grounding yourself in the present moment. Spend a few minutes in this relaxed state, taking deep, calming breaths.

Step 7: Complete the Journey

When you're ready, slowly open your eyes and wiggle your toes and fingers. Bring your awareness to everything around you. Allow yourself to fully experience the sense of relaxation throughout your entire body. Take your time, don't rush.

Step 8: Reflect

Take a moment to reflect on how you feel after this exercise. Notice any changes in your physical and emotional state?

By consistently incorporating this practice into your daily routine, you'll not only experience immediate benefits but also nurture a deep sense of self-awareness. It allows you to identify and effectively manage the triggers of stress and emotional responses. Engaging in PMR fosters an enhanced understanding of your thoughts, feelings, and physical sensations, further connecting you with your genuine self. This skill set can prove invaluable in an environment where demands are high and emotions run deep, ultimately guiding you through your college journey with resilience and grace.

Reflection Questions

1. Reflect on a moment during your college experience when embracing your authentic identity presented a challenge or an opportunity. How did mindfulness, or the lack thereof, impact your response and its outcome?

2. Consider the concept of "leaning in" to moments of discomfort mentioned in the text. Can you recall a time when encountering diversity or new ideas in college caused defensive discomfort? How did you navigate that experience, and what did it reveal to you about your values and beliefs?

3. How does mindfulness practice contribute to shaping a more inclusive and diverse college environment, and in what ways can students implement these practices to become active agents of change both on campus and beyond?

4. In what practical ways can mindfulness be integrated into daily campus life to actively combat the 'isms,' and how can it contribute to a sustainable culture of empathy, respect, and equity in a college setting?

5. How can mindfulness serve as a common ground for all students, regardless of their background, dealing with college stressors?

Chapter Two

C's Make Degrees

In the world of higher education where the pursuit of knowledge and self-discovery is combined with the pressures of academics and the demands of personal growth, college life is a complex journey. This journey is marked by exhilarating highs and effing terrible lows, and at its heart, this journey often boils down to one thing – performance. As students, we often find ourselves wrestling with the relentless waves of performance stress that includes test anxiety, heavy responsibilities, time management challenges, final exams, projects, and more. In this chapter, we explore the concepts of college stress, and navigate the rough seas of uncertainty and self-discovery that so many of us face during college.

We also offer a personal story of Alyssa, a girl who reflects upon the diverse challenges students encounter, from the sleepless nights spent worrying about finals, to the weight of responsibilities that accumulate like textbooks on a shelf. Her journey through the maze of college, and her battle against test anxiety, time constraints, and the countless hours dedicated to school-work, offer a relatable lens through which we can examine our own experiences.

Amid the chaos of college life, it's essential to remember that college is not just about test scores and assignments – it's about growth, both personal and academic. Higher education is a place where mistakes are not only accepted, but actively encouraged, as a means of learning. It's a space where we find ourselves, discover our passions, and develop resilience. This chapter aims to unravel the secrets to navigating college life successfully, reminding you that each stumble along the way is a vital part of the journey. With this insight, we seek to empower you with tools to confront the stresses of university life and emerge stronger, wiser, and more mindful individuals.

Within these pages, you will find not only the experiences of students like Alyssa, but also explore the art of mindfulness, offering you a "Quieting the Mind Meditation" as a beacon to help you navigate the challenging sea of intrusive thoughts and negativity. We encourage students to build their own strategies and practices, from mindfulness to reflection, to establish a greater sense of balance, well-being, and success in college. Remember, everyone's college experience is unique; so find what works for you. As we embark on this journey together, you'll discover the power of meditation to ease the chaotic storms within your mind. Join us as we explore the transformative potential of mindfulness and how it can lead you to success and well-being during your college years and beyond.

Alyssa's Story

To begin, Alyssa, a determined and compassionate young woman, set her sights on a dream that was anything but ordinary. Her journey through college was marked by the goal of attending Vet School, a passion that she had since childhood. Her fascination with animals, their well-being, and the strong feeling to make a difference in their lives, were the driving forces that fueled her academic pursuits. Alyssa's journey mirrors the boundless dreams that college students harbor and the trials they face as they strive to turn these dreams into reality. Personally, for Alyssa, undergrad life meant not only budgeting time for school, but also juggling work commitments and enduring a daily hour-long commute to campus, a challenge that only added to the weight of her academic journey.

One of the biggest challenges Alyssa confronted was the persistent grip of test anxiety. The looming thought of exams, with their high stakes and weighty expectations, cast a shadow on her academic path. The anxiety was not a subtle sensation; it was a debilitating occurrence before every significant test. The sleepless nights leading up to exams, the racing heartbeats, and the pervasive fear of failure became her unwelcome companions. It was a battle she fought not only for herself, but for the animals whose lives she aspired to improve. In her words, "I felt like I physically didn't have the time to prepare sufficiently for tests sometimes, no matter how much time I committed to studying." The pressure was almost too much.

Alyssa's academic journey was a balancing act of too many tasks like coursework, laboratory responsibilities, and extracurricular activities. The magnitude of these responsibilities often weighed on her, threatening to obscure the path she had passionately chosen. With each assignment, each lab report, and each responsibility, the pressure intensified. The sacrifices she made were not for her alone, but for the countless animals that depended on her future success. As she puts it, "Even if I had a 4.0 GPA, I didn't have enough vet experience hours or farm hours to get into vet school either." She had to continue to work non-stop to reach her goal, budgeting her time efficiently.

Her unwavering dedication and tireless efforts in pursuit of her dream to attend vet school ultimately paid off. Fueled by her deep passion for animals and her commitment to making a difference in their lives, she embarked on the challenging journey of applying to numerous vet schools across the country. Her rigorous academic pursuits, countless hours spent accumulating vital veterinary experience, and the relentless battle against test anxiety all served as testaments to her perseverance. While her academic journey was marked by challenges, setbacks, and the weight of immense responsibilities, her resilience never failed. After navigating the demanding process of vet school applications, Alyssa received the much-awaited acceptance letter from one of the schools she had applied to. Her hardearned success illuminated the path she had chosen with strong determination and unfaltering grit, proving that dedication and passion can lead to the realization of any dream. Alyssa's story serves as an inspiring reminder that perseverance and tenacity can open doors to a future brimming with opportunities, where dreams are realized, and passions become a lifelong purpose.

But her success came at the expense of stress, broken relationships, and not much of a social life. Reflecting back on her four years of undergrad, Alyssa now realizes she spent her time so stressed out about the future that not much of those years comes back to her easily. Looking back, she can't remember nearly as many of those days as she wishes. On top of that, her singular determination for academic success, she now realizes, was an easy excuse to not take care of the other parts of herself like love and a social life. During college, her relationships, both friendships and love interests, were interrupted and hindered as she would always turn away to refocus on school work. She still wonders what might have happened if she'd felt motivated to balance school success with dating or a social life. She looks back and realizes all the fun parties she missed because her anxiety over the next day was pre-venting her from being present on "this" day. You get our point.

Along her college journey, marked by the weight of responsibilities and test anxiety, Alyssa endured under-grad school without the aid of mindfulness practices. In hindsight, she realized that the "Quieting the Mind Meditation" and similar techniques could have been helpful tools for maintaining balance and focus while in the face of academic pressures, her demanding daily commute, and the pursuit of crucial vet experience hours. Alyssa's reflection serves as an obvious reminder of the many untapped resources within the college ex-perience, which is now motivating her continued quest for academic and personal success. She also offers priceless advice to her fellow student peers, encour-aging them not to repeat the mistakes she made by not knowing about these mindfulness techniques. Her message is clear: explore these practices, for they will provide the balance and strength needed to thrive in the face of academic challenges.

Alyssa's story serves as a beacon of hope but also a word of caution, reminding us that college is not just about acquiring knowledge and success, but also about personal growth in all aspects of your life, build-ing resilience and taking care of yourself. Even though she didn't have the knowledge on how to incorporate mindfulness practices in her earlier college years, she persevered through the physical and mental challenges of her journey. Her determination and love for animals carried her through. Now, having learned about the power of mindfulness, she sees a way to ease the struggles that defined her early college experience. Alyssa is committed to implementing mindfulness techniques in the future during Vet School, recognizing their potential to provide the inner strength and balance needed to thrive in the face of academic challenges. Her journey, much like other countless college students, teaches us that even without prior knowledge, one can find the resilience to persevere, and with newly discovered wisdom of mindfulness, there's potential to face the future with greater ease and purpose. We must embrace the challenges of college with an open heart and remember that the journey of self-discovery is worth every high and low along the way.

Fear of Failure: Embracing Mistakes

The fear of making mistakes can be an ever-present shadow, especially when it comes to grades and tests. College life, with its demanding academic standards and the relentless pursuit of excellence, often leaves – what many think of as – very little room for errors. The pressure to achieve high grades and excel in every project can create a culture of fear around making mistakes. Students are often conditioned to believe that

any misstep or imperfect grade can have dire consequences on their academic and future professional
lives, especially if it is their very first C.

Perfectionism: a relentless pursuit of flawlessness. We
all know what I am talking about, right? The constant
need to go above and beyond, looking over every little
detail to simply attain that perfect grade. Do not worry,
it is a burden that many college students carry. Perfectionism is a mindset that we all endure which can lead
to crippling anxiety and stress. The belief that anything
less than perfect is a failure takes a toll on mental and
emotional well-being. The paradox of perfectionism is
that, while it aims for excellence, it often results in increased fear of making mistakes and can hinder personal growth, hurting grades.

Embracing mistakes can be a daunting concept for college students. We know this is not an easy suggestion,
yet it is a critical part of the learning and growth process. Mindfulness encourages us to be present in the
moment, to accept things as they are, and to embrace
the imperfections of life, including our own. Mindfulness teaches us that making mistakes is a natural part
of being human, and it is through these mistakes that
we learn and grow. As a matter of fact, an NCBI study
showed that 35% of people who do practice mindfulness do so in order to reduce stress. By practicing
mindfulness, students can develop a healthier relationship with their own errors, viewing them not as failures,
but as opportunities for growth.

Mindfulness invites students to shift their perspective on mistakes. Rather than seeing them as failures, they can be viewed as valuable lessons. Every misstep is a chance to learn, adapt, and improve. No individual is perfect, right? Mindfulness encourages students to approach their mistakes with curiosity and self-compassion, rather than self-criticism. It allows them to acknowledge their errors without dwelling on them and to move forward with a greater sense of resilience. Test grades do not define you!

Embracing mistakes, with the aid of mindfulness, ultimately becomes a path to success and well-being. It transforms the college experience from a relentless pursuit of perfection into a journey of self-discovery and growth. Mindfulness equips students with the tools to navigate the academic challenges of college with ease and strength. By letting go of the paralyzing fear of mistakes, students can free themselves to explore, learn, and become the best versions of themselves. Embracing mistakes is not a mark of failure; it is a testament to the courage to grow, the wisdom to learn, and the strength to thrive in the dynamic world of higher education.

Building Self Confidence: Reflection

In the fast-paced and demanding environment of college life, taking a moment to reflect can seem worthless. Pause for a second, yes – right now – and breathe. Try to remember the last time you paused to simply breathe. Feels good, right? You're welcome.

You just allowed yourself to take a moment to reflect. Reflection is a valuable tool for personal growth and well-being. It's a pause in the constant stream of academic and personal commitments that allows students to gain perspective on their experiences, decisions, and emotions. Consider if you have taken a moment to reflect on your college journey? What are the most significant experiences or decisions you'd like to explore through reflection?

The journey through college is often characterized by a whirlwind of experiences, from challenging coursework to the creation of new friendships to the pursuit of dreams. Within this storm of activity, it can be easy to lose sight of the bigger picture. Reflecting on one's journey helps students reconnect with their goals, values, and the reasons they embarked on this educational path. Take a moment to reflect on your initial goals when you started college. What were they originally? Now having been on campus, how have your experiences developed or changed those goals?

Mindfulness practices play a significant role in enhancing the power of reflection. By being fully present in the moment, students can sharpen their self-awareness and develop a deeper understanding of their experiences. Mindfulness encourages students to engage in self-reflection without judgment, allowing them to explore their thoughts and emotions without fear of criticism. This builds self-confidence that can transfer into the classroom setting. Have you tried mindfulness practices to aid your reflection? How have they influenced your self-awareness and the way you approach self-reflection?

Mindful reflection allows students to make sense of their college experiences, not only the successes, but also the setbacks and challenges. It offers an opportunity to celebrate and learn from both achievements and struggles. This practice can lead to a greater sense of self-compassion and resilience, which are vital tools for navigating the ups and downs of college life. As you engage in mindful reflection, what have you learned from your setbacks or challenges, and how have they contributed to your personal growth and resilience?

Incorporating reflection into your daily life, with the support of mindfulness, paves the way for you as a college student to find success and well-being. It's a practice that helps all students make informed decisions, manage stress, and maintain a sense of balance throughout their journey. Mindful reflection isn't just about looking back; it is about preparing for the future with a clearer understanding of oneself, one's goals, and the ways to overcome challenges. What steps will you take to incorporate reflection and mindfulness into your daily life, and how do you envision these practices contributing to your success and well-being in college and beyond?

Coping Mechanisms: Meditation

College life is filled with opportunities for self-discovery and personal growth, while also having unique challenges. Amidst the hustle and bustle of academics, responsibilities, and final exams, students often find themselves struggling with the question of how to effectively manage the pressures of college stress that we have introduced. Coping mechanisms emerge as valuable tools in addressing this question.

One powerful coping mechanism that we explore in this chapter is meditation. Meditation is a mindfulness practice, like deep breathing, which offers a haven of stillness amidst the chaos. We're guessing since you made it to college, you have a sense of what meditation is, but just in case: meditation is a practice where an individual uses a technique, such as focusing the mind on a particular object, thought, or activity, to train attention and awareness, and achieve a mentally clear and emotionally calm and stable state. It has been practiced in cultures all over the world for thousands of years.

Meditation has an ancient and varied history, deeply rooted in the religious and spiritual traditions of the East, particularly within Hinduism and Buddhism, where it has been practiced for over 5,000 years. Early Hindu scriptures, the Vedas, contain references to meditative techniques, while Buddhist texts outline various forms of meditation, such as Vipassana (insight meditation) and Samatha (concentration meditation). Over millennia, these practices spread across Asia, each culture adding its own interpretations and methods. In the 20th century, meditation underwent a renaissance as it encountered Western interest, leading to scientific research on its benefits and the secularization of the practice, which has removed or reduced spiritual elements to focus on mindfulness and stress reduction.

Typically, a session begins by finding a quiet space and adopting a comfortable position to help minimize distractions. As one enters into meditation, there is often an effort to reign in the wanderings of the mind, to bring your attention towards a single point of focus, such as the breath or a mantra. Gradually, this concentration turns into a state of deep absorption, where the usual barrage of thoughts begins to subside, and a sense of mental clarity and tranquility emerges. The boundaries of the self can feel less distinct, allowing for moments of profound connection with the present moment. Emotionally, there can be a sense of expansive peace, and an encounter with feelings of joy or compassion. This experiential journey is often not linear, peppered with ebbs and flows of focus, and is typically something that deepens with practice over time.

Meditation encourages students to be fully present in the moment, allowing them to release the grip of anxiety and stress. Mindfulness meditation equips students with the tools to cope with the challenges of test anxiety, heavy responsibilities, and time management hurdles. Mindfulness expert Jon Kabat-Zinn claims that "Mindfulness is the final common pathway of what makes us human, our capacity for awareness and for self-knowing." He also believes that mindful meditation helps to refine this process of paying attention. Through meditating, students can reframe their relationship with stress and experience a greater sense of well-being. Students can also find comfort in reflection, which provides students with a space to make sense of their experiences, celebrate achievements, and learn from setbacks. It is a tool that fosters self-compassion and resilience. By reflecting on their college journey and implementing meditation, students can identify patterns of success and moments of growth, allowing them to face challenges with greater wisdom and perseverance in the future.

Chapter Two

Benefits of Meditation

Meditation is a transformative practice that offers a profound impact on both mental and physical well-being. It involves training the mind to focus, to find stillness, and to cultivate a heightened sense of awareness. This ancient practice has made its way into the modern world and will (hopefully) find a special place in the lives of college students seeking a path of balance and strength. Among the various meditation techniques, "Quieting the Mind Meditation" stands out as an effective method for calming racing thoughts and reducing stress.

College life often comes with many stressors – from deadlines and exams to personal responsibilities. We are all familiar with these headache-causing aspects of our new college lives, maybe even which have started in our junior and senior years of high school. "Quieting the Mind Meditation" acts as a soothing balm for the mind, enabling students to alleviate the burdens of stress. By learning to be present in the moment and to let go of the grip of anxiety, this specific meditation technique helps students find a sense of calm in the college life commotion.

The demanding academic environment of college forces a need for strong concentration and focus. This meditation practice offers a powerful tool for enhancing these cognitive abilities. Through regular practice, students sharpen their mental acuity, making it easier to study, retain information, and conquer exams. The specific practice of "Quieting the Mind Meditation" allows students to cultivate an inner sense of clarity and attention.

Meditation goes beyond reducing stress. It also nurtures emotional well-being. It encourages students to connect with their emotions, embrace self-compassion, and find a sense of balance. By learning to observe their thoughts and feelings without judgment, students can develop a healthier relationship with their inner self. This can lead to increased self-esteem, resilience, and a more positive outlook on life. Meditation not only equips college students with the tools to navigate the challenges of college life. By embracing the practice of meditation, students are not only better prepared to face the academic and social rigors of college but also to thrive in the complex world beyond.

Exercise: Quieting the Mind Meditation

Follow these steps that guide you through a basic mindfulness meditation practice, helping you focus on your breath, acknowledge your thoughts without attachment, and become more present in the moment.

Step 1: Find a Quiet and Comfortable Space

Begin by finding a quiet and comfortable space where you won't be disturbed. You can sit in a chair with your feet flat on the ground or on a cushion with your legs crossed, whichever is more comfortable for you.

Step 2: Relax Your Body

Close your eyes gently and take a few deep breaths to help relax your body. Inhale slowly and deeply through your nose, and exhale through your mouth. Let go of any physical tension with each exhale.

Step 3: Focus on Your Breath

Shift your attention fully to your breath. Pay close attention to the natural rhythm of your breathing. In through your nose. Out through your mouth. In through your nose. Out through your mouth. Feel the air entering your nostrils as you inhale and leaving your body as you exhale. Pay attention to the sensations as the cold air enters your body and then warm air leaves your body.

Step 4: Acknowledge Your Thoughts

Keep breathing. Keep breathing. As you breathe, you may notice thoughts arising. This is perfectly normal. When a thought comes to mind, simply acknowledge it without judgment. Imagine your thoughts as passing clouds in the sky and let them drift by without clinging to them. Let's take the next several minutes to simply breathe, letting your thoughts pass by as they occur. Simply breathe.

Step 5: Label Your Thoughts

Take a moment now to check in with your thoughts. Was there a particular thought that showed up more than once? What kind of thought was it? For the particularly persistent thoughts, you can give it a brief label, such as "worry," "planning," or "doubt." Try not to address the content of the thought, but the form. What kind of a thought is it or was it? Name them, and let them pass.

Step 6: Return to Your Breath

After labeling your thoughts, gently guide your focus back to your breath. Bring your awareness back to the sensations of the air going in through your nose and out through your mouth. Concentrate on the rise and fall of your chest, belly, or the sensation of your breath at the tip of your nose.

Step 7: Observe Sensations

Notice any other physical sensations you may be feeling in your body. Does something on your body hurt? Do you feel warm or cold in one place or another? Is there a part of you that feels uncomfortable, or, pleasurable? Pay attention to areas of tension and draw your breath towards those places, imagining the release of the tension with the release of each breath.

Step 8: Continue for a Set Time

Continue to focus on your breathing for a set amount of time, such as 5, 10, or 15 minutes, depending on your comfort level and availability. Try not to be concerned with how long you're meditating; the key is the quality of your practice and your presence with your breath. Find a rhythm and practice with your breath that suits you. Perhaps count each breath. Or, focus on manipulating the location of each breath. Do what makes most sense for you.

Step 9: End Mindfully

When you're ready to conclude the meditation, slowly bring your awareness back to the present moment. Gently open your eyes, look around, wiggle your fingers and toes, and take a few final deep breaths. Thank yourself for taking time for yourself today.

Daily Schedules: Putting it All Together

"Quieting the Mind Meditation" is not just a practice; it's a way to transform your relationship with stress and improve well-being.

Start Slow: Remember, as with any new habit, it's important to set realistic goals. Start with a manageable duration for your meditation sessions, perhaps just five to ten minutes. Gradually increase the time as you become more comfortable with the practice. This approach allows you to integrate meditation into your daily routine without feeling overwhelmed. Next, designate a quiet and comfortable space for your meditation practice. This can be a corner of your room, a cozy chair, or a cushion on the floor. Personalize it with items that bring you a sense of calm, such as candles, soothing music, or a favorite blanket. Make this space inviting and conducive to your meditation journey.

Stay Steady: Keep in mind, consistency is the backbone of a successful meditation practice. Commit to meditating regularly, whether it's daily, a few times a week, or according to your schedule. Set reminders on your phone or use meditation apps to help you stay on track. The more consistent you are, the more you will benefit from the practice.

Experiment: Do not forget that every individual's meditation journey is unique. We are all different! Feel free to experiment with variations of "Quieting the

Mind Meditation," or something completely different, and find what works best for you. Whether it's using a guided meditation app, incorporating a specific mantra, or trying walking meditation, be open to adapting the practice to suit your needs. The key is to make it your own and enjoy the journey of self-discovery and well-being that meditation can provide.

YOU GOT THIS: A Call to Action

As we conclude this chapter, it's essential to reflect on the transformative power of mindfulness and "Quieting the Mind Meditation." The college experience is a dynamic journey, one filled with highs and lows, challenges, and triumphs. Mindful meditation has been proven to be effective in multiple studies, maybe it's time for you to hop on the trend yourself. Heck, maybe you could be the new rising Tik Tok star who teaches meditation to everyone on the app!

Throughout this chapter, we've explored the complexities of college life, from the pressures of academics to the demands of personal growth. College is more than just a degree or a grade; it's an opportunity for personal growth and self-discovery. It's a place where you are allowed to make mistakes and learn from them. The pressures of performance stress may feel overwhelming at times, but they are an inevitable part of the journey. The ups and downs are all threads in the fabric of your story. You must learn how to manage them.

We encourage you to take action. You have learned about the benefits of mindfulness, the "Quieting the Mind Meditation" technique, and practical steps to implement them in your daily life. Now, it's time to apply these valuable tools to your own college journey. This book is your call to action! Remember:

- Start Today: There's no better time to begin your mindfulness practice than now. Whether you're a college student or someone supporting a college student, commit to incorporating mindfulness into your daily life. Start with short meditation sessions and gradually expand them.

- Be Patient and Persistent: Mindfulness is a skill that grows with practice. Don't be discouraged if your mind wanders during meditation or if you face challenges along the way. Persistence is key.

- Explore Your Resources: There are countless resources available to support your mindfulness journey. From meditation apps to books, online courses, and local mindfulness communities, you have a wealth of tools at your disposal.

- Share Your Journey with Others: Consider sharing your experiences and insights with fellow students, friends, faculty, or family. Discuss the benefits of mindfulness and meditation with others, as it can be a source of inspiration and support.

As you stand at the threshold of your college journey, it's crucial to recognize the profound impact that mindfulness and the "Quieting the Mind Meditation" can have on your experience. College life is a time of discovery, self-improvement, and challenges, often marked by intense periods of academic demands, personal growth, and inevitable moments of stress. In these closing thoughts, we dive deeper into the wisdom of integrating mindfulness into your college journey.

One of the most powerful lessons you can take from your college experience is the acceptance of your imperfections. It's okay to make mistakes, to falter, and to learn along the way. Embracing your imperfections doesn't mean lowering your standards; it means recognizing that growth often arises from setbacks. Mindfulness teaches you to approach your journey without self-criticism and judgment. It enables you to view your challenges and achievements as integral parts of your personal evolution.

Mindfulness invites you to engage fully with the present moment. In college, it's easy to get caught up in the past, dwelling on past failures or achievements, or to be preoccupied with the future, worrying about upcoming exams or career prospects. The present moment is where your life unfolds, and mindfulness allows you to savor it. It's a practice of being fully present in your studies, your interactions with friends, and even in the solitude of your own thoughts.

Resilience is a quality that defines your capacity to face adversity and emerge stronger. Mindfulness equips you with the tools to develop resilience. As you navigate through the highs and lows of college life, the ability to bounce back from challenges becomes a powerful asset. Mindfulness encourages a mindset of adaptability and flexibility, helping you find strength even in the most demanding moments.

College often feels like a whirlwind of commitments and responsibilities. Mindfulness provides a sanctuary of balance within imbalance. It's a way to center yourself when everything around you seems to be chaotic. When you bring mindfulness into your daily life, you create a haven of serenity where you can return, a place that helps you maintain equilibrium and well-being even in the face of unavoidable pressures.

While striving for academic excellence and personal growth, it's easy to forget about self-compassion. Mindfulness encourages you to treat yourself with the same kindness and understanding that you would offer to a close friend. It reminds you that mistakes and imperfections are a part of your human experience, and that self-compassion allows you to heal and grow.

Your college journey doesn't end with a degree or graduation. It extends far beyond those milestones. Mindfulness and the "Quieting the Mind Meditation" technique offer you not just tools for college life, but for the journey of life itself. According to Benefit News, in 2016, 22% of companies had mindfulness progress, demonstrating its popular spread into the workforce. As you embrace your imperfections, discover the present moment, and harness resilience and balance, you set a course for a life rich in self-awareness, resilience, and well-being.

As you embark on this remarkable journey, consider the wisdom of mindfulness. Integrate it into your daily life, use it to find balance in imbalance, and nurture your spirit with self-compassion. As Kabat-Zinn says, "The adventure that the universe of mindfulness offers is one possible avenue into dimensions of your being that may have perhaps gone ignored and unattended or denied for too long." Allow mindfulness to become your lifelong companion, a source of strength, clarity, and wisdom, that will guide you through college and beyond with grace and success. Remember, C's still get degrees, so take a deep breath, and have a mindful minute.

Reflection Questions

1. What have you learned most about yourself through reflection of your college experience so far? Are there changes to be made? Things to improve on? Things to keep the same?

2. How have learning about academic stress and embracing mistakes changed how you will approach the next struggles of college life that you will face?

3. Which mindfulness practices have you tried? Are they influencing you to be more self-aware and take time to self-reflect? Should you try a new practice?

4. From what you have learned regarding your personal reflection, have you applied them to help you grow as a student and embrace your college experience?

5. What steps will you commit to in order to incorporate mindful meditation and reflection into your lives to help contribute to your success and well-being in college and beyond? Who will you share this new advice with?

Chapter Three

Treat Yo'Self

Welcome to a chapter that's all about you, the college student navigating the depths of academic challenges, social expectations, and personal growth. It is in moments like these that self-care becomes both an elusive luxury and a dire necessity. We understand the pressures and uncertainties that can come with college. The good news is that you're not alone. We're here to offer guidance and support.

In these pages, we'll explore the transformative power of self-care through mindfulness, providing the essential tools that can empower you to thrive during your college years. Keeping that in mind, various meditation practices will be mentioned that will help guide you in your journey to self-care, such as the Body-Scan Meditation practice waiting for you at the end of this chapter. This meditation will help you when you're struggling to sleep, and restart your mind and body back to square one. Mindfulness meditation, as John Kabat-Zinn refers to it, is an openhearted, moment-to-moment, non-judgmental awareness that involves intentionally focusing one's attention and concentration on a particular object, thought, or experience. It is a skill that encourages a state of deep inner reflection and calm, promoting self-discovery, emotional balance, and a profound connection to the present moment.

We'll also explore the downsides of unhealthy self-care through a personal anecdote and how the Body-Scan Meditation practice could have benefited that person in that situation. We're not here to add more items to your to-do list, or overwhelm you with academic jargon. Instead, we're here to help you discover the art of balancing your academic and personal life, fostering healthy habits, as well as finding your unique path to well-being.

We want you to understand that well-being is not just a distant goal; it's a journey that begins with small, practical steps that you can take today. Whether you're a seasoned self-care enthusiast or a newcomer to the concept, there's much to learn and apply. We'll provide you with insights and practical tips to help you incorporate mindfulness into college life and make the best choices for your well-being as a student. With the knowledge shared ahead, you have the compass to steer your college experience towards well-being, no matter where you stand in your self-care voyage. Your well-being matters, and we're here to help you make it a priority.

Healthy & Unhealthy Self-Care

As a college student it's so easy to continue bad habits. Let's be honest, some of them are *Really. Hard. To. Break.* We get it. But that means that binge watching Netflix, procrastinating on your calculus homework, or locking yourself in your dorm all day, need to end. No judgment, but we have to reel it in.

In this section, we're going to explore the difference between healthy and unhealthy self-care practices – a crucial distinction that can make or break your college experience. You see, self-care isn't just about bath bombs and spa days, as delightful as those may be, it's a holistic approach to nurturing your physical, emotional, and mental well-being. It's about making choices that uplift you, boost your resilience, and enable you to thrive, even in the midst of academic L's and an identity crisis. However, it's crucial to understand that not every self-care approach holds the power to refresh and uplift your spirits. There are strategies that truly rejuvenate and fortify, and though there are habits that may provide temporary relief, ultimately it will drain your energy and leave you feeling even more stressed.

Overworking & Overcommitting

We all have high expectations of ourselves that can lead us to being overwhelmed by trying to accomplish them. As Ash Ketchum from Pokemon says, we want to be the very best, but where do we draw the line? The pressure to excel academically, while maintaining an engaging social life, and perhaps even holding part-time jobs, can lead to a hectic schedule that leaves little room for self-care. Constantly pushing yourself to the limit without taking breaks or time for relaxation can lead to burnout, physical health issues, and poor mental health. Once we hit rock bottom, it's impossible to believe that there is a way to come back up. Including simple practices such as learning how to say "No," taking breaks, prioritization, achieving balance, and overall accepting your limitations will help you put yourself first.

First of all, do not feel bad about simply saying "No." Your friends, family, roommates, professors, or opportunities that you come across on campus, should not be prioritized above your well-being. If you are aware that you're committing to something where you will not put 100% in, you are already spreading yourself thin. Those two letters hold power, so use it to your advantage and view it as your special weapon to protect your inner peace. For instance, saying "No" whenever your friends invite you to a party you don't want to go to, or when you are feeling forced by peers to join new clubs and organizations. Another instance is when your manager asks you to cover a coworker's shift at work. Despite wanting to accomplish everything, don't be afraid to decline additional commitments knowing your schedule is already full. Practicing how to say "No" is creating a personal boundary for yourself. With mindfulness meditation, such as the Body-Scan, you can approach commitments with a clear mind, assess whether they align with your goals, and decide whether they are worth your time and energy. When you struggle to say "No," you are unintentionally adding more work, leading to increased stress, diminished personal time, and ultimately neglecting your emotional well-being. Putting yourself first is an important step towards self-care. Mindfulness meditation encourages self-awareness, and helps you recognize your own limits, priorities, and values. By practicing mindfulness, you become more attuned to your true desires and what is genuinely important to you.

Isolation

Some days, all we want to do is stay inside and never see the light of day ever again. We get it, we really do. But, as the authors of a self-care chapter, it's important we shed light on the negative effects of isolation. Although those first moments of alone quality time can feel refreshing, doing it consistently, especially day after day, can impact your relationships, increase stress, limit social skills, and decrease self-esteem. This is a result of the fact that you are missing out on positive feedback and affirmation from social connections. Social connections create a sense of belonging and acceptance, which is fundamental to mental and emotional well-being.

Feeling connected to a community or group can boost self-esteem as human beings need connection to thrive. The relationships that we create amongst ourselves increase our well-being by having emotional support and creating a sense of belonging. Talking to friends, family, or peers can help you share your feelings, concerns, and experiences, reducing the emotional burden of isolation.

How you can expand your social network during college is by attending campus events, joining clubs and study groups, as well as engaging with your roommate, classmates, and academic advisors. Although this can be a challenge to some people, keep in mind that college should be an experience where you are trying to find yourself, which means you have to step out of your shell. Mindfulness teaches you not to be attached to specific outcomes in social interactions. This can alleviate performance anxiety and help you focus on the process of connecting with others rather than seeking validation or approval. Remember that building social connections takes time. Be patient and open-minded as you meet new people. Don't be discouraged by initial setbacks or rejections; persistence is often key to building lasting relationships.

Procrastination

Procrastination is a habit that many college students are familiar with, often being seen as a form of a way to take a break, or a means of temporarily escaping academic pressure. While it may offer momentary relief, procrastination is essentially an unhealthy form of self-care with numerous negative consequences. At first glance, procrastination might appear to be a simple delay tactic. As Jon Kabat-Zinn states, "If we start to pay attention to these impulses as they arise, we may find that we are virtually addicted to distracting ourselves." It seems harmless to put off studying, working on assignments, or other responsibilities for a little while. After all, taking a break is often encouraged in the context of self-care. However, the critical distinction lies in how this time is spent. Procrastination typically involves engaging in mindless activities or distractions rather than genuinely relaxing or recharging. Procrastination becomes unhealthy when it turns into hours of aimlessly scrolling through social media, binge-watching TV shows, or engaging in other unproductive behaviors. So the next time you find yourself procrastinating with a super important task, remember that you could be engaging in mindful practices that will increase your productivity and awareness.

So, how can mindfulness help college students, like you, break free from the cycle of procrastination? Instead of watching that TV series, you can incorporate Body-Scan meditations during your study breaks. This practice can benefit you by letting your mind relax and rest. Mindfulness is about being fully present in the moment, and this practice can significantly enhance your ability to overcome procrastination. Other mindful breaks, such as mindful journaling or mindful walks, can be effective ways to recharge, and return to your responsibilities with a clear and focused mind. This mindful approach to self-care not only alleviates stress but also empowers you to tackle tasks with greater efficiency, satisfaction, and relief. The overwhelming amount of assignments can feel like the walls are closing in, but don't let yourself be the victim of mindless procrastination.

Integrating mindfulness practices into the pursuit of your goals makes them more meaningful, achievable, and aligned with your values. When you set specific goals you gain clarity about what you want to achieve, create a sense of purpose, as well as increase motivation. One can apply SMART goals: Specific, Measurable, Achievable, Relevant, and Time-bound. By setting SMART goals, you can break these tasks into smaller, more manageable steps that allow you to be present in the moment. It's easier to take that first step when you know it's not a mountain, but instead a small hill. When you set deadlines for completing tasks related to your goals, you hold yourself responsible for meeting those deadlines. Self-accountability can be attained by including mindfulness into your goal-making process. Mindfulness can lead you to be more conscious of what needs to be completed with self-accountability, not self-criticism. This self-accountability can be a powerful deterrent against procrastination. When you can see how far you've come in achieving your goal, it provides a sense of accomplishment and reinforces your motivation to continue.

When you have a clear goal in mind, you're less likely to wander off the path and procrastinate with mindless activities. By incorporating mindfulness into your goal-setting process, you not only increase the likelihood of achieving your goals, but also form a deeper connection to your aspirations. It promotes a sense of purpose and fulfillment in the pursuit of your objectives, making the journey as important as the destination.

Eating Habits

College life can sometimes lead to erratic eating habits, from late-night study snacks to rushed meals between classes. Several factors such as our emotions, energy levels, and stress will lead to mindless eating. Although it may feel nice to distract ourselves with Snickers bars and Ben and Jerry's ice cream whenever we get dumped or too stressed, eating your emotions away won't feel as nice after the food parade. In addition, the accumulation of lack of sleep from days where you've stayed up late to work on assignments, picking up late shifts, or from going out with friends can lead to mindless eating. Consistently having those times, when you scarf down whatever's left in your fridge or school backpack when you might already be full and energized, leads to unhealthy eating habits.

Mindful eating can be a game-changer in promoting good health or even preventing procrastination induced by poor energy levels and concentration. Mindfulness eating means enjoying a meal wholeheartedly. Yes – that means putting down your phone or any sort of distractions. This practice includes being aware of the taste and texture of your meal, simply being present with each bite, maybe laughing along with loved ones. Enjoying a meal can be challenging since everyone has a goal in how one wants their body to look. Mindful eating encourages a shift of focus from external appearance to internal well-being. Nourishing your wonderful body is self-care. We need to learn that food is a source of nourishment, pleasure, and cultural connection. Incorporating mindfulness into your eating habits can be a powerful step toward nurturing a healthier relationship with food and promoting self-compassion. When you take a moment to ask yourself why you're eating, you're cultivating mealtime mindfulness. This is crucial as it enables you to be purposeful in your eating, guaranteeing that you're not simply consuming food out of sheer boredom. Remember, savoring each bite lets you enjoy the experience of having a meal.

Practicing mindfulness in your food choices extends to the way you approach grocery shopping. Attending university may be the first time you go out on your own to do food shopping. Though the grocery store may feel like a boring errand, it's actually a great place to practice mindfulness. Take the time as you walk down the aisles to take in the variety of colors on display, the smells from fresh produce, the noises you hear, and the textures of food you inspect. Simple practices such as these can give your mind a break from an overwhelming week at college.

Balancing Work & Play

Balancing work and play in college is like walking a tightrope, and trust us, it's the secret sauce to a killer college experience. You've got your coursework – those assignments, exams, and late-night study sessions that make or break your GPA. But here's the thing: college life isn't just about the grind. It's a time to explore, make friends, and grow into the person you want to become. Finding the right equilibrium is a delicate yet essential endeavor. It is a dynamic process, where you will learn to allocate your time wisely, dedicating yourself to your studies while also savoring moments of relaxation and recreation. It involves the creation of effective time management skills and the establishment of clear priorities. But, mindfulness can better help facilitate both aspects of the college experience so that we don't have those FOMO (Fear of missing out) moments.

Mindful time management allows you to allocate time, not only for your studies, but also for projects, hobbies, and aspirations that bring you fulfillment. Mindful time management is the practice of allocating your time with intention and awareness. It's about making conscious choices that support your academic and personal goals while ensuring you have time for relaxation and play. First, learn to prioritize what is important and put that on top of your list of tasks, then create a schedule using mindfulness that allows you to thrive academically and personally. Mindfulness can help you set limits and recognize the signs of burnout. Being aware of when you are feeling overwhelmed will then let you know that there needs to be a modification to your schedule by tuning in to what you need. For instance, you can practice mindful journaling where it can be used in a non-judgmental way to destress and simply reflect on your accomplishments, or what needs to be done. You can take these pockets of time to reflect on your limitations and learn to accept them without judgment. Focus on your own challenges and goals without worrying about competing with your peers or feeling like you're falling behind.

A mindfulness practice can also enhance the rejuvenating effects of your leisure. It might seem like work to be intentional about sitting down and meditating for fifteen minutes when you're comfortable in bed relaxing, but the effort matters. Weirdly, sometimes it takes effort to truly allow your body, mind, and spirit to rest. These small but consistent acts of mindfulness can reduce the accumulation of stress and improve your overall well-being. It's about embracing mindful time management as your key to a thriving college life. Balance your academics and your personal pursuits, reduce stress, and conquer your daily tasks. Your college journey is about more than just surviving; it's about thriving. Enjoy every moment, and make the most of it!

Positive Sleep Schedules

With late-night study sessions, social activities, and the ever-tempting allure of Netflix (or "Netflix and Chill" ;)), it's easy to neglect proper sleep. However, establishing and maintaining positive sleep schedules is a cornerstone of well-being. As college students, your brains are constantly absorbing and processing information, which makes sleep even more vital. A well-rested mind is focused and more likely to be productive and be present in the moment. With the help of the Body-Scan meditation, us college students will be better equipped to establish a healthy nighttime routine, ensuring that we designate a time in our day to rejuvenate our minds and bodies after a long day of classes and dealing with people.

To enhance the quality of your sleep, aim to establish consistent sleep patterns. Going to bed and waking up at the same time every day, even on weekends, helps regulate your body's internal clock. There is also the importance of adding elements before going to bed. For instance, dimming the lights, limiting screen time before heading to bed, having a comfortable bedroom, and limiting caffeine or alcohol intake. Little things like these can train your body for when it is time to go to sleep. When you prioritize quality sleep, you'll find it easier to concentrate on your studies and manage your responsibilities effectively. If sleep is a constant struggle, don't hesitate to seek support from your college's counseling services or a healthcare professional. By understanding the significance of quality sleep, you can implement positive sleep schedules and meditation exercises such as Body-Scan Meditation, to enhance your sleep with a well rested mind. Adding the Body-Scan Meditation can help you be better equipped to tackle the challenges of college life as well as have a clear and focused mind.

Amaris's Story

We want to take a page or two now to share with you the story of Amaris, a 2023 college graduate student, whose experience really demonstrates the difficulties of college and how those difficulties can impact our sleep.

Amaris's college journey began at Scripps College in California and later continued at the University of Houston (UH), which was marked by unexpected challenges. The initial excitement of attending Scripps was overshadowed by health issues that were worsened by an irregular sleep schedule. Amaris would experience extremes, either sleeping for close to two days straight, or squeaking by with less than four hours of rest per night. This relentless anxiety, stemming from a solitary transition to a new state without the comfort of established friendships, made it difficult to focus on academics. While Amaris excelled in a small writing class, earning an A due to the intimate setting and a strong desire to perform well, the lack of sleep led to a significant struggle with early morning Chemistry classes, which resulted in a failing grade.

Chapter Three

Upon transferring to the University of Houston, Amaris began working with a tutoring service, a job that, despite its noble mission, compounded the stress of academic life. The commitment to assisting 'tier 3' students was immensely rewarding yet emotionally draining. This role, coupled with a major and minor that demanded extensive reading, research, and writing, further complicated time management. Amaris's studies often extended late into the night, leading to difficulty with early mornings and diminishing the enthusiasm for the valuable work being done in local elementary schools.

The cumulative effect of these responsibilities started to take a toll on Amaris's well-being. The effort to balance work and study often left little room for self-care, exacerbating the sense of burnout. Despite the hurdles, Amaris persevered, demonstrating resilience in navigating the demanding dual roles of student and educator. The experience tutoring, though taxing, also instilled a deep sense of accomplishment and purpose, enriching Amaris' understanding of the real-world applications of education.

However, the mounting pressures eventually necessitated a reassessment of priorities. Amaris began to carve out time for rest and self-reflection, recognizing the importance of mental and physical health in academic success. Efforts were made to structure a more sustainable routine, one that accommodated the rigors of university life while also allowing for much-needed recuperation. This adjustment period was a learning curve, not just in the academic sense but also in life management, as Amaris worked to strike a balance between the pursuit of educational goals and the maintenance of health and wellness.

Improving Mental Health

College life is a thrilling and transformative journey, marked by intellectual growth, new friendships, and exciting opportunities. Yet, for many students, it's also a time of immense academic pressure, heightened stress, and the need to juggle multiple responsibilities (like mentioned in the previous chapter). In the pursuit of excellence, mental health can often take a backseat, leading to anxiety, depression, and overwhelming stress. But mindfulness really does offer a response.

As you should know by now, mindfulness is a state of openhearted and non-judgmental awareness, characterized by a deliberate and focused presence in the current moment. Jon Kabat Zinn describes meditation as "a gesture of the heart that recognizes our perfection even in our obvious imperfection, with all our shortcomings, our wounds, our attachments, our vexations, and our persistent habits of unawareness." It involves paying full attention to one's thoughts, feelings, bodily sensations, and the surrounding environment without attempting to change or judge them. This age-old practice, rooted in the art of self-care and self-awareness, holds the key to unlocking a deeper sense of well-being and mental resilience. In this section, we'll explore its profound impact on college students' mental health.

Mindfulness, at its core, fosters a compassionate and non-judgmental relationship with oneself. Mindfulness can play a pivotal role in supporting and enhancing mental health among college students, and the numbers reflect its significance. According to the American College Health Association, over 60% of college students report experiencing overwhelming anxiety, while almost 40% experience depression that is so severe it becomes difficult to function. Mindfulness meditation has been shown to significantly reduce symptoms of anxiety through breathing, a way students can gain greater control over their anxiety or stress.

Yes, meeting new people, taking exams, and complicated relationships are all stressful and can create anxiety, but when it comes to situations like this, remember to take a deep breath. In fact, take one right now, by using the mindful box breathing technique, literally called "Box" breathing, you'll become one step closer to integrating mindfulness in your everyday routine.

Exercise: Box Breathing

Step 1: Find a Quiet Place

Locate a quiet and comfortable place where you can sit or lie down. Ensure you won't be disturbed for a few minutes. Sit with your back straight or lie down with your hands resting on your abdomen. Close your eyes if you feel comfortable doing so.

Step 2: Take a Breath

Start by taking a deep breath in through your nose for a count of four seconds. Feel the air entering your lungs and expanding your abdomen as you inhale.

Step 3: Pause

Once you've taken a full breath in, pause and hold your breath for a count of four seconds. During this pause, focus on the stillness and the sensation of having your breath contained. Exhale slowly and completely through your mouth for a count of four seconds.

Step 4: Exhale

As you breathe out, release any tension or stress you're holding onto. After you've exhaled completely, pause and hold your breath for another four seconds. Use this moment to experience the stillness and absence of breath.

Step 5: Repeat

Continue this box breathing pattern for a few minutes, or for as long as you need to feel more relaxed and centered. Inhale for four seconds, hold for four seconds, exhale for four seconds, and hold for four seconds before starting the cycle again. Throughout the practice, keep your attention on the sensation of your breath. If your mind wanders, gently guide your focus back to your breath. Do this for as long as you feel you need to.

Box breathing can be a powerful tool to use whenever you're feeling overwhelmed by anxiety or stress. It helps slow your heart rate, reduce tension, and promote a sense of mindfulness and relaxation. Practice this technique regularly, and it will become an invaluable resource for managing the challenges of college life.

Mindfulness can help manage and alleviate symptoms of depression. While it's important to note that mindfulness is not a replacement for professional treatment, it can complement therapy and medication. Mindfulness encourages you to become aware of your thoughts and emotions without judgment. This self-awareness can help you recognize depressive thought patterns and emotional triggers. Mindfulness practices teach you to accept your emotions without resistance. This leads to improved emotional regulation and a decrease in the intensity of depressive emotions. Instead of self-criticism, you can offer understanding and support to yourself.

A mindfulness practice that can help alleviate depression is called "Lovingkindness Meditation," which will be explained more in depth in Chapter Five, "Situationships." This practice is designed to promote self-compassion, positive emotions, and a sense of connection to others and yourself. It can be particularly beneficial for individuals dealing with depression by cultivating feelings of kindness and reducing self-criticism. Regular practice can gradually improve your overall mood and contribute to managing depressive symptoms.

It's essential to remember that mindfulness is a skill that takes practice – this is why it's called a "meditation practice." Consistency is key to experiencing its full benefits. If you're dealing with depression, consider seeking guidance from a mental health professional. They may even be able to help you incorporate mindfulness into your treatment plan. Mindfulness, when practiced regularly and in conjunction with other therapeutic approaches, can be a powerful ally in your journey towards better mental health and well-being.

Additional Outlets of Self-Care

We wanted to leave you with variations of mindfulness practices below that you can use on your journey of self-care, because we believe that self-care can come in all shapes and sizes. Use these variations of mindfulness whenever you need to improve your self-care routine:

- Mindful Journaling: Mindful journaling can be a powerful practice for college students to gain clarity, reduce stress, and foster self-awareness. It provides a space for self-reflection and helps you navigate the challenges and triumphs of your college journey with greater mindfulness and resilience. It helps you focus on a specific aspect of your college experience that you'd like to explore further. It could be an academic challenge, a personal goal, a relationship, or simply how you're feeling on that particular day.

- Mindful Exercising: Mindful exercising is the practice of engaging in physical activity with full awareness and presence in the moment. It involves focusing on the sensations, movements, and breath involved in the exercise, while letting go of distractions and worries. Mindful exercise promotes a deeper connection between the body and mind, enhancing the overall experience and often leading to reduced stress and increased well-being. How many of you have gone on a run and hated every second of it? That's mindful running, lol. How many of you go running and repeat a mantra or count your breaths across each mile? That's mindful running, too. Mindful exercise can be applied to a wide range of physical activities, from yoga and meditation, and strength training, making it a versatile approach to improving both physical and mental health.

- Music Meditation: Music meditation is a practice that invites individuals to immerse themselves in the profound world of sound, using music as a vehicle for mindfulness, relaxation, and self-discovery. In this meditative journey, the individual selects a piece of music that resonates with their emotions, preferences, or intentions. The chosen music can be instrumental, nature sounds, classical compositions, or any genre that speaks to the soul. Take a moment and head to Spotify or Apple Music, and search for "meditation music." Some of our favorites are the Solfeggio Frequencies and Binaural Beats.

Exercise: The Body-Scan Meditation

When times are rough, and sleep schedules are all over the place, it's important to resort to mindfulness to gauge your mind and relax your body. Body-Scan meditation can be a valuable tool for college students struggling with their sleep schedules in particular. This mindfulness practice can help students relax, alleviate physical tension, and quiet their minds, which can contribute to better sleep. The Body-Scan Meditation is a simple yet powerful technique that can help you release physical and emotional tension. Here's a step-by-step guide on how to practice it effectively:

Step 1: Find a Quiet Space

Begin by finding a quiet, comfortable space where you won't be disturbed. You can practice this meditation either sitting in a chair with your feet flat on the floor or lying down on your back with your arms at your sides. The choice is yours, but ensure you're in a position that feels relaxed yet alert.

Step 2: Start with Deep Breaths

Before you begin the Body-Scan, take a few deep breaths to settle into the present moment. Inhale deeply through your nose, allowing your abdomen to rise as you fill your lungs, and then exhale slowly through your mouth. These deep breaths will help you become more centered and focused.

Step 3: Begin at the Top

Close your eyes, if you're comfortable doing so, and bring your attention to the top of your head. Imagine a gentle beam of light or warm energy slowly moving down from the crown of your head.

Step 4: Focus on Each Body Part

As this imaginary beam of light or energy moves down, pay close attention to each part of your body it touches. Start with your head and face, moving through your neck, shoulders, arms, chest, and back. Notice any areas of tension, discomfort, or sensations as you go.

Step 5: Breathe into Tension

When you encounter areas of tension or discomfort, take a moment to breathe into them. Inhale deeply, and as you exhale, visualize and feel the tension releasing. Imagine it melting away with your breath.

Step 6: Continue Downward

Continue moving your attention down through your abdomen, hips, thighs, knees, calves, and all the way to your feet. Explore each part of your body, scanning for any areas of tightness or discomfort.

Step 7: Non-Judgmental Observation

Approach each sensation and body part with non-judgmental observation. If you encounter discomfort, refrain from labeling it as "good" or "bad." Instead, simply observe it and allow it to be as it is.

Step 8: Bring Your Mind Back

Throughout the practice, your mind may wander or get distracted. That's okay; it's a natural part of meditation. When you notice your mind has drifted, gently and without self-criticism, bring your focus back to the Body-Scan.

Step 9: Take Your Time

Body-Scan Meditation should be practiced slowly and mindfully. There's no rush. The entire process might take 15-30 minutes, or even longer if you wish. The key is to be fully present and attentive.

Step 10: Conclude Mindfully

When you've reached your toes, take a few moments to experience your body as a whole. Notice how you feel after completing the scan. You might feel more relaxed, lighter, and in touch with your body.

Gradual Return: When you're ready to conclude the meditation, bring your awareness back to the room. Take a few more deep breaths to transition back to your everyday state of mind.

Or,

Prepare for Sleep: After completing the Body-Scan, you can gently return your attention to your breath. This can help you drift off to sleep. By understanding the significance of quality sleep and implementing positive sleep schedules and habits, you'll be better equipped to tackle the challenges of college life with a clear and focused mind.

Regular practice of a Body-Scan meditation before bedtime can condition the body and mind for better sleep. Mindfulness practice makes it easier to relax and fall asleep, especially for college students, like former student Amaris, who often faced sleep challenges due to academic and lifestyle factors.

Transformative practices like the Body-Scan Meditation can offer students, like you, an invaluable toolkit to navigate the challenging times of higher education. In the pursuit of academic excellence, personal growth, and a fulfilling social life, it's easy to lose sight of our own well-being, both mentally and physically. This is where self-care and mindfulness come into play. Mindfulness, remember, is being in a state where you are non-judgmental of yourself while also being present in the moment. Therefore, it is important to incorporate mindfulness to offer yourself a profound sense of clarity and presence, allowing you to fully engage with the moments that shape your college experience and your life beyond. This chapter has illuminated the path toward a healthier, happier, and more balanced college experience through self-care mindfulness. As college students with diverse backgrounds and experiences, we understand the unique pressures and demands you face daily. Yet, we also see your potential for growth, resilience, and fulfillment. By embracing self-care mindfulness, you can transform your college journey into a time of self-discovery, empowerment, and well-being.

Reflection Questions

1. How would you describe your current self-care practices, and do they align with the healthy self-care practices discussed in this chapter?

2. Can you identify specific situations or triggers that tend to challenge your self-care and mindset? How might mindfulness help you navigate these challenges?

3. What is one self-care practice or mindset shift you are committed to incorporating into your daily routine after reading this chapter?

4. Consider the personal anecdote shared in this chapter about the graduated college student. Can you relate to any aspects of her experience?

5. What steps will you take to foster a more mindful and self-aware approach to your daily activities and interactions with others?

Chapter Four

IYKYK

College has always been a pivotal time for personal development, where we encounter ideas, form lasting relationships, and undergo unique experiences. However, the current generation of students has faced a unique twist. You stand at the intersection of traditional academic rigor and the digital revolution, making your journey even more complex and multifaceted. The devices in your hands as students are both gateways to limitless knowledge and potential black holes of distraction. The gateway to limitless knowledge can lead to being indulged in doom scrolling. While social media platforms provide opportunities for connectivity and self-expression, they also come with risks such as comparison, cyberbullying, and distorted reality. These devices can become addictive as you become dependent on likes, subs, and messages.

This is when the profound and immediate value of mindfulness truly shines. When mindfulness becomes more important in your college life, you begin to ask yourself questions such as:

- Is this social media post a genuine reflection of who I am or what I value?

- Does this online debate merit my energy and attention?

- Do I feel happier after I scroll through social media than I did before?

Integrating mindfulness into your life can provide clarity in previously confusing areas. Firstly, it increases your focus towards academic and college pursuits. By being present and fully engaged in studies, students can absorb information more effectively, leading to improved attention span and comprehension. Discussion topics become more meaningful, and the learning process transforms into a joyous journey rather than being instinctual or unneeded.

In personal relationships, mindfulness plays an equally crucial role. As students navigate friendships, mentorships, and romantic relationships, being present ensures that each interaction is meaningful and genuine. By actively listening and expressing themselves with authenticity, students can build bonds that are both deep and enduring.

Additionally, technology, with its vast number of platforms and meaningless notifications, can make it hard to have beneficial online interactions. But with mindfulness as an anchor, you can stay grounded and be more aware of your connection with social media. This will allow you to differentiate between meaningful content and mere noise, ensuring a balanced and healthy digital consumption pattern.

One of the most overlooked aspects of the college experience is self-growth and reflection. It's a pivotal period where lifelong values, beliefs, and principles are being challenged and shaped. By integrating mindfulness, you can embark on this inner journey with a clear vision, charting a path of continuous growth and self-improvement. With the implementation of mindfulness into the lifestyle of college students, mindfulness has an increased impact on navigating and crafting a college experience that is both enriched and valued.

Social Media

College students like you are living in two worlds at the same time: the traditional one with all the studying, and a new digital one that moves at the speed of light. Your phone is like a tiny magic window to everything. It's great for finding stuff out, but it can also make hours disappear. Social media lets us chat with friends and show off what we're doing, but it's not all fun and games. Sometimes it makes you feel low if you're comparing yourself to others. You might find yourself creating a version of yourself on the internet, and might need to take a moment to ask, "Is that really me?" or, pause to remind yourself that people tend to only put the best parts of their lives on social media. Being mindful helps you stay 100% in the moment, whether it's when you're hitting the books or having a heart-to-heart.

Jon Kabat-Zinn throws us a real question: "With all this talk about connectivity, what about connectivity to ourselves? Are we becoming so connected to everybody else that we are never where we actually are?" He's saying we might be getting tricked into feeling close to people on our screens, but actually, we're just scrolling non-stop, which can make us feel left out. This is what people call "FOMO," or the Fear of Missing Out. You see your friends having fun, and it can sometimes sting. It's okay to not be a part of everything, everywhere - the key is to make moments that are important to you.

Social media is all about dopamine, that thing in your brain that makes you feel good when something "fun" happens. Social media uses this by giving you little unpredictable rewards that keep you coming back. Beyond this, it's like a jungle of other issues. First, there's Distorted Reality Perception, where the cool stuff people post online makes your real life seem boring. The loss of real-life chats that are replaced by quick digital ones, with too much info hitting you all at once. Second, there's Emotional Contagion, where negativity spreads like wildfire online. Finally, the biggie, Digital Dependence, which is exactly what you think. These social media issues can trap you into thinking everyone else's life is perfect and yours isn't, which unbalances the concept of being mindful. You end up looking for likes instead of looking inside yourself. If you don't watch out, this can mess with your ability to focus and make you emotionally hooked on your screen.

So yeah, college life is this big mix of old and new stuff to deal with. Every swipe, every lecture–it's all painting this picture of your student life. But if you keep mindfulness in your back pocket, you can stride through all this with your head up, smiling, making a college story that's worth telling.

Peer Pressure

Peer pressure is a subtle force that can sway our choices, nudging us towards actions that may be inconsistent with the ones you've made before. It's not just the over-the-top dares or direct challenges from friends; peer pressure can manifest in quieter, more insidious ways. For instance, the constant showcase of experiences on social media can create a silent nudge, urging us to join in, not just in the fun, but sometimes in the risk-taking behaviors that seem to be the ticket to acceptance – like attending every party, or experimenting with alcohol or substances.

The quest for validation is deeply woven into the college tapestry. It's an unspoken desire for recognition and acceptance that can drive students to chase after certain ideals or behaviors. Kabat-Zinn reflects deeply on this when he says, "Yet for all our desire for recognition, to be seen and known and accepted as we are, and to have that be recognized as a basic human right, how easily we can be ensnared by our own limited and self-centered thinking." Kabat-Zinn is touching on the irony of seeking external validation when what we truly need is to feel valued and accepted for who we genuinely are.

Often, the pursuit of validation can lead to a change in behavior. Some may find themselves turning into people they barely recognize – partying excessively, engaging in reckless behavior, or even subtly changing their speech to garner more attention. This search for validation can sometimes be a mask for underlying insecurities, and in the quest to fill that void, individuals may find themselves engaging in a pattern of actions that, in the end, bring little genuine satisfaction.

The trap of social media adds another layer to this complex scenario. Observing friends immersed in what appears to be non-stop excitement can stir a sense of urgency to participate, driven by the belief that popularity and happiness are measured by followers and likes. But this is a false reality that often leads to a cycle of comparison and dissatisfaction.

To break free from this cycle, it's essential to step back and reflect – does this relentless pursuit of validation truly contribute to personal growth and happiness? It's here that mindfulness can save the day. By engaging in mindfulness, we can start to question our motives and behaviors. Have we drifted from those we care about due to these pursuits? Mindfulness practices, suggested at the end of this chapter, offer a pathway to reconnect with our authentic selves, to evaluate what actions truly contribute to our well-being and happiness.

In practicing mindfulness, we learn to ask the right questions: Are these activities genuinely fulfilling? Do they align with our core values and who we want to be? If they don't, it's a sign to reevaluate, to seek satisfaction not in the short-term applause of peers, or the digital thumbs-up of social media, but in the nurturing of our true selves. This introspection is not just about avoiding negative behaviors, but about fostering self-care and awareness, recognizing the real from the reflected, the substantive from the superficial. It's a journey towards a deeper, more resonant form of happiness that comes from within.

Body Image

The college experience is often depicted as a time of self-exploration and newfound independence. Yet, it can also be a period where body image concerns intensify, due to social expectations and media portrayals. Students from all walks of life, regardless of their background or field of study, may find themselves grappling with body image issues. These are caused by many components, including social media influences, the search for peer validation, and the prevalent social expectations within the college environment. The quest for self-acceptance becomes tangled within a web of external pressures, making the college years a critical time for addressing and mitigating these pervasive concerns.

Body image issues do not discriminate; they affect students of all genders, races, and socioeconomic statuses. The transition to college life often brings with it an increased focus on appearance as students like you navigate new social circles and confront the perceived standards of attractiveness. These issues are compounded by the developmental stage of emerging adulthood, where identity is still in flux and the opinion of peers holds considerable weight. In this crucial phase, the pursuit of an 'ideal' body image can overshadow the importance of health and wellbeing.

Chapter Four

Social media serves as a highlight reel, showcasing curated lives and idealized bodies, which often distorts reality and sets unrealistic standards. The typical college student's daily consumption of social media can lead to constant comparisons, with each scroll through a newsfeed potentially diminishing self-esteem. Social expectations within the college scene amplify this issue, as students may feel pressured to match the physically appealing portrayals they see online with their real-world presence. This can spur a vicious cycle of self-scrutiny and the relentless quest for approval through 'likes' and comments, wrongly equating physical appearance with personal worth.

Mindfulness, the practice of intentional and nonjudgmental awareness of the present moment, offers a powerful counterbalance to these pressures. It encourages an inward turn away from external validation, fostering self-compassion and an appreciation for one's body as it is, rather than as social media makes it look like it should be. By promoting an authentic connection with oneself, mindfulness can dismantle the harmful belief that self-worth is dependent upon adhering to social expectations of beauty. This shift in perspective, from external validation to internal acceptance, is pivotal in forming a healthy body image.

The journey through college is just as much about acquiring knowledge as it is personal growth and self-discovery. Integrating mindfulness into this journey allows students to combat the negative impacts of social media and societal standards on body image. By valuing their bodies for their functionality and the experiences they enable, rather than solely for their appearance, students can cultivate a sense of bodily agency and self-respect. The mindful college student, therefore, emerges not only with academic proficiency, but with the ability to appreciate their own unique physical make-up, unattached from the standards of society. In the end, mindfulness doesn't just alleviate body image issues. It empowers individuals to navigate their college years with a profound and abiding sense of self-validation.

Partying

Parties are one of the highlighted parts about college. Whether they're intimate gatherings among friends and family or a huge frat party, they allow for letting loose and having lots of fun. Parties offer a moment for people to showcase their most genuine selves, and sometimes, their most unpredictable faces. There are many types of parties for those seeking excitement and entertainment. From lively bars and pulsating clubs, to cozy restaurants, captivating live music venues, and enchanting theaters. Your preferences may lean towards an adventurous night out at clubs with exhilarating live music events, or perhaps you prefer a more relaxed evening, indulging in the magic of plays or musicals. In the familiar company of friends and loved ones, it's often easier to be yourself. There's a sense of comfort and security that comes from being surrounded by those who understand and accept you for who you are. You can let your guard down, be spontaneous, and let your true personality shine. However, there's an equally important aspect of social growth, and that's the ability to be yourself in the company of new people.

When stepping into the unfamiliar territory of a party, mingling with people you've never met, the dynamics change. It's a place where you might find yourself navigating undiscovered social waters, and this can be both exciting and challenging. Here, being yourself means finding common ground, being courteous, and projecting a version of yourself that is open to new connections. The key is to strike a balance between authenticity and adaptability, allowing your genuine self to shine through while also being attuned to the expectations and social cues of the moment.

Parties have a way of bringing out both the best, and even the worst in people. While they create opportunities for memorable moments and genuine connections, they can also initiate unexpected behavior. It's often the presence of alcohol and drugs that acts as the catalyst, pushing some students to extremes they might not otherwise explore. These substances can, at times, serve as a double-edged sword, removing inhibitions and filters that usually temper our words and actions. They have the power to reveal hidden parts of people's personality, making them more exuberant and open, while leading others down a path of recklessness. It's in these moments that the true essence of a person may become apparent, for better or worse.

Whatever your choice, always remember that your safety should be a top priority.

When you venture into bars and clubs, it's important to be aware of your limits, especially when it comes to alcohol and drugs. Despite what you might think, these places are not always safe. Some people attend nightlife events with the intent of exploiting vulnerable individuals. To protect yourself, ensure that your drink is in a safe location and being watched by someone you trust.

One golden rule of nightlife is strength in numbers; using the buddy system. Going out with trusted friends and companions significantly decreases the likelihood of becoming a target. Having a support network of people who watch out for each other can make all the difference. There's great strength in numbers, so you can enjoy your night out knowing that you and your friends are looking out for one another.

It's also essential to understand that you always have the choice to "stay in." Like mentioned previously, it's OKAY to say, "No." You should never feel pressured to go out if you're not in the mood. Your friends will understand and respect your decision. Your well-being is the top priority, and it's perfectly okay to pick a quiet night in when you're not up for a night in the town.

Alcohol

The encounter with alcohol in college is almost thought of as a rite of passage, and understanding its multifaceted nature is crucial for any student. Alcohol comes in various forms, each with its own character and potency. From liquors to wines and beers, these beverages play diverse roles in social settings and possess varying levels of alcohol-by-volume (ABV). As students embark on their college journey, they often encounter many new experiences, including the complex world of alcohol. While alcohol can enhance social gatherings and even offer some health benefits when consumed in moderation, its varied forms and ABV percentages present a challenge for the inexperienced. Mindfulness, the practice of purposeful, non-judgmental attention to the present moment, can be an invaluable tool in navigating these experiences. This section explores how mindfulness can inform and transform one's relationship with alcohol, especially within the dynamic setting of college life.

The spectrum of alcoholic beverages ranges from the distilled spirits like gin, vodka, and whiskey to the brewed varieties such as beers and wines. Under-

333

standing these differences is crucial. Liquors, with their higher ABV, and liqueurs, enhanced with flavors from fruits and spices, offer a more intense experience than the softer, more gradual influence of beers and wines. With beers being a staple in college due to their accessibility and affordability, and wines offering a diversity from the robust reds to the lighter whites, students are often at the crossroads of making informed choices about consumption.

ABV serves as a guide to the strength of different alcoholic beverages. Light beers, with their lower ABV, make a common appearance at college gatherings, while the potent nature of craft beers, high-ABV wines, and spirits requires a more cautious approach. Cocktails, too, can deceive with their fluctuating ABVs, making mindfulness in consumption essential. Being aware of how different drinks affect the body and mind, and recognizing one's limits, is a practice in mindfulness that can prevent the negative consequences of overconsumption.

Moderation is key when alcohol enters the social scene. Mindfulness encourages a presence that heightens the enjoyment of social interactions without relying on alcohol. The gentle buzz of a few beers may facilitate conversation, but mindfulness reminds us to value the connection rather than the consumption. Similarly, while a glass of antioxidant-rich red wine might contribute to a healthy heart, mindfulness urges a balance that ensures these benefits do not tip into the detriments of simply too much.

The practice of mindfulness offers a reflective pause in the vibrant and often overwhelming world of college drinking. It encourages students to savor the moment and the flavors of diverse alcoholic beverages without falling prey to their intoxicating effects. By promoting an understanding of one's responses to different types of alcohol and their ABV levels, mindfulness fosters a conscious, responsible approach to alcohol consumption. Thus, as students navigate the new situations that college life presents, mindfulness can be their ally, ensuring that their experiences with alcohol, from the casual beer to the complex cocktail, are both enjoyable and harm-free.

Marijuana

As marijuana strides through the evolving gateway of legality across various states and countries, its presence on college campuses is more common than ever. The shift from prohibition to acceptance has seen this once-vilified substance rebranded in some quarters as a wellness product, complete with potential therapeutic benefits. Heck, they even have forms of it for animals! In college, a time traditionally associated with experimentation and self-discovery, students often navigate their own personal relationship with marijuana, exploring its recreational allure alongside its capacity for abuse and its place in certain wellness practices. This section presents an impartial exploration of marijuana's presence on campuses, acknowledging its potential for both responsible and harmful use.

The changing legal status of marijuana signifies a shift in social perceptions, with many college students coming of age in an era of reduced stigma around its use. Legality varies widely, creating a patchwork landscape where the substance may be treated as a commonality in one region and as contraband in another. This legal contradiction complicates the conversation, as students from different jurisdictions may bring diverse perspectives and experiences to the college setting. Regardless of its legality, the dialogue around marijuana on campus is becoming more prominent, with a growing emphasis on informed choices and awareness of legal implications.

Marijuana's journey into the mainstream includes an important narrative on the difference between responsible use and abuse. College is often a time where boundaries are tested, and this is true for marijuana consumption as well. While some students may opt for occasional, recreational use that does not interfere with their studies or social responsibilities, others may find themselves struggling with moderation, facing the detrimental effects of habitual use. Acknowledging this spectrum is crucial in fostering an environment where informed decisions are made, and support is available for those who need it.

For some, marijuana transcends its recreational use, intertwining with their spiritual and religious practices, even complementing mindfulness routines. This incorporation can range from seeking enhanced spiritual awareness to using the substance as a tool for meditation and stress relief. In such contexts, marijuana is approached with reverence and intentionality, starkly contrasting with its more casual or recreational consumption. Within college life, this demonstrates the diverse roles that marijuana can play in individual practices and beliefs, contributing to the broadening spectrum of its use.

Marijuana's presence in college life is proof of a larger cultural and legal transformation. As attitudes toward marijuana continue to evolve, it becomes the responsibility of educational institutions to encourage a dialogue that emphasizes legality, safety, and the importance of making informed choices. Colleges are reflections of the wider world, where the complexities of marijuana use – and its potential for both benefit and harm – must be navigated with care and consideration. The task then is not to cast judgment, but to encourage a new and improved understanding of marijuana's place in the college experience, recognizing its potential for responsible use, the reality of its abuse, and its unique role in certain cultural and wellness practices. This balanced discourse can equip students with the knowledge to approach marijuana with a critical and mindful awareness that will serve them during their college years and beyond.

The Hard Sh*t

College life can be a crossroads of exploration and a period of vulnerability, where students may encounter the seductive edge of hard drugs. While the enjoyment with such substances like cocaine, ecstasy, and heroin may seem tempting in certain social situations, they are fraught with dangers and the potential for addiction. Yet, in the face of these risks, mindfulness emerges as a beacon of resilience, offering a grounding force and a pathway back to well-being. This section considers the complex relationship between the practice of mindfulness and the experimentation with hard drugs during the college years, touching upon the compassionate understanding necessary for those who may stumble along this precarious path.

The college environment can, for some, become a backdrop for experimentation with hard drugs, which may be driven by curiosity, peer influence, or the desire to escape stress. The consequences of such experimentation are extremely dangerous, with the threat of addiction and adverse health effects looming large. It's imperative to approach this reality with compassion rather than judgment, recognizing the challenges students face and the pressures that may lead to risky behaviors. Mindfulness does not condone this exploration but offers a lens of empathy towards those who find themselves entangled.

Mindfulness can help ground you against the tides of addiction. By fostering self-awareness and stress management, mindfulness can empower students to make more conscious choices and potentially resist the interest towards harmful substances. For those already struggling, mindfulness practices can be a stepping stone in the journey of recovery, helping to regain control and nurture a healing focus on the present.

While traditionally cast as "hardcore," psychedelics like LSD, Ketamine, and Psilocybin are undergoing a renaissance in scientific research, showing promise in treating conditions like depression and PTSD. These substances are powerful tools of the mind that, under controlled and supervised conditions, can offer therapeutic breakthroughs. It's crucial to distinguish between this emerging field of medicinal use and the unregulated use of these drugs, which remains illegal and potentially hazardous. In any context where such substances are explored, it is vital for safety and well-being that sober supervision is present.

In the journey through college and the potential encounters with hard drugs, mindfulness stands as both a preventative measure and a remedial practice. As the narrative around certain psychedelics shifts towards therapeutic potential, it remains a testament to the importance of context, intention, and respect for the potency of these substances. Above all, the cultivation of mindfulness can instill students with the inner strength to navigate their experiences with wisdom and care. In recognizing the vulnerabilities and pressures of college life, the ultimate aim is to foster an environment that prioritizes informed decision-making, safety, and compassion – principles that uphold the integrity of the individual's journey through these years.

Jerome's Story

Jerome's journey through the prestigious halls of an Ivy League college was as impressive as it was predictable for someone of his caliber. Acclaimed for his intellect and his relentless pursuit of academic excellence, Jerome found himself navigating a world where achievements were king, and he was royalty. But beneath the sheen of success was a quieter, less visible Jerome – one that wanted to be more than just his grades and reputation.

As the semesters rolled by, Jerome stumbled upon a new ritual – drinking. It wasn't just about the buzz or the fleeting warmth of liquid courage. It was an exploration, a discovery of a side of himself unrestrained by expectations. With every drink, he felt liberated, finding a way to socialize that was new to him and intriguing.

However, with the shadows of family history lingering in the corners of his mind, Jerome's relationship with alcohol began to weigh on him. The drinks that once felt like liberation slowly morphed into a necessity, a requirement to be the life of the party, the version of himself that he barely knew, but everyone else loved. As junior year came to an end, a creeping sense of unease settled in. Jerome was no stranger to the dangers of addiction, and the last thing he wanted was to walk that thin line.

It was during this time of introspection that Jerome found an ally in a professor – someone whose wisdom stretched far beyond the classroom. In a candid exchange, Jerome expressed his concerns, clarifying he didn't believe he was an alcoholic, but that his drinking needed to be slowed down. The professor, understanding the crossroads at which Jerome stood, offered a simple mantra: "I am enough. I am me. I am valuable in my own skin."

Skepticism initially clouded Jerome's mind, but desperation for a change encouraged him to give it a try. Sitting down, eyes closed, he let the words roll off his tongue, feeling them resonate within. Surprisingly, the exercise sparked something – a sense of self-assurance that didn't require a glass in hand. He carried this mantra with him, a whispered chant at parties, a silent affirmation before social engagements, until it became second nature. This was his "Buddha courage" – the strength to stand firm and genuine without the deceptive comfort of alcohol.

Jerome didn't just practice this mantra through the remainder of his college days. It became a cornerstone of his life, a source of unwavering strength that guided him past graduation and into his early career. Meditation replaced the bottle, not as a cure but as a conscious choice. Looking back, Jerome didn't see his college drinking as a battle fought and won, but as a detour on his path to self-discovery. He acknowledges the role alcohol played, but more importantly, he cherishes the daily meditation that continues to remind him that indeed, he is enough.

Exercise: Social Confidence Affirmations

Social media and real-life social interactions can often create waves in our mental and emotional wellbeing. This mindfulness exercise is designed to act as an anchor, grounding you amidst the challenges of peer pressure, body image concerns, and the desire to fit in. On social media, peer pressure forms the urge to conform to the lifestyles and values portrayed by others. Offline, this pressure continues at social gatherings, compelling us to act against our better judgment. The constant bombardment of idealized images can erode self-esteem and skew our perception of body image. Both online and offline, the desire to be accepted can lead us to mask our true selves, resulting in a disconnect between who we are and how we present ourselves to the world.

Here's an exercise, designed for a duration of 5-10 minutes, which incorporates breathing techniques and affirmations. This guide is adaptable for various settings, whether at a party or alone in a dorm room. The exercise helps to build confidence, maintain personal boundaries, and cultivate a light-hearted approach to social interactions and social media.

Step 1: Find a Comfortable Position

Sit or stand in a comfortable position. If you're at a social event, find a quiet corner. If you're in your room, choose a peaceful spot.

Step 2: Focus on Your Breathing

Close your eyes gently. Take deep, slow breaths. Inhale through your nose, feeling your diaphragm expand, and exhale through your mouth. Concentrate on the rhythm of your breathing for a minute.

Step 3: Affirmation for Confidence

Inhale and mentally say, "I inhale confidence and strength."

Exhale and think, "I exhale doubt and fear."

Repeat this affirmation three times.

Step 4: Affirmation for Boundaries

Inhale and say to yourself, "I respect my limits and needs."

Exhale and affirm, "I let go of the need to please everyone."

Repeat this three times.

Step 5: Affirmation for Light-Heartedness

Inhale, thinking, "I embrace this moment with lightness."

Exhale, saying, "I release the weight of others' judgments."

Do this three times.

Step 6: Return to Normal Breathing

After completing the affirmations, return to your natural breathing pattern. Observe any changes in your thoughts or feelings.

Step 7: Gentle Acknowledgement

Open your eyes slowly. Acknowledge the effort you've made to address your social anxiety. Remind yourself that this is a process, and every step counts.

Step 8: Re-engage at Your Own Pace

Whether you're at an event or contemplating social media, re-engage at a pace that feels comfortable for you. Remember, you're in control.

Additional Tips:

If you're in a social setting and can't close your eyes, maintain a soft gaze and focus internally.

These affirmations can be altered to suit your personal needs or specific situations.

Consider practicing this meditation regularly, ideally at a consistent time each day, to reinforce its benefits. But most importantly, keep it in your pocket for those times you begin to feel overwhelmed, out-of-place, or unable to concentrate during social activities. Remember, the goal of this exercise is not to eliminate social anxiety completely but to manage it in a healthy way, empowering you to engage with others and with social media more mindfully and confidently.

Reflection Questions

1. How has mindfulness impacted my ability to manage stress and improve my overall well-being, and how can I incorporate it more effectively into my daily routine?

2. How does my relationship with alcohol impact my overall well-being, and am I making responsible choices when it comes to alcohol consumption?

3. When was the last time I felt shame because my body image didn't live up to a standard being set by friends or social media? When this happens again, what mindfulness resources can you use to confront and process those feelings of shame?

4. How do I handle peer pressure in various aspects of my life, and what strategies can I employ to assert my values and make decisions in alignment with my principles?

5. In what ways does social media influence my choices and well-being, and how can I maintain a healthy balance between online and offline life while using social media more consciously?

Chapter Five

Situationships

Sofia's Story

After a long day of studying and classes, Sofia sat crying in her dorm room. The heated words that had passed between her and Jordan, her boyfriend, played on repeat in her head. They had always been deeply in love and shared countless cherished memories. However, as college life became increasingly demanding and hectic, their relationship began to suffer. Stress from exams, assignments, and part-time jobs was taking a toll on both of them. Small misunderstandings grew into significant arguments, and they found themselves drifting apart. Sofia worried that their once-strong connection was slipping away.

Getting advice from a friend, Sofia decided to attend a mindfulness workshop in an attempt to calm her anxious thoughts. Her constant stream of worries about the future and regrets about the past were clouding her interactions with Jordan. When in conversation with Jordan, Sofia began practicing active listening. Instead of planning responses or getting lost in her thoughts, she focused on truly understanding what Jordan was saying. She also began to practice something called a Lovingkindness meditation (discussed later in this chapter). In a Lovingkindness meditation, a person offers blessings and well-wishes to others from afar. Sofia started doing this before bed each night. Active listening and meditating in a way that included some attention to Jordan, allowed her to better empathize with her partner's feelings and concerns.

One evening, after a particularly heated argument, instead of reacting defensively or emotionally, Sofia took a few deep breaths to center herself and brought mindfulness to the forefront. She acknowledged her own feelings and asked Jordan to share his perspective as well. This open and non-judgmental conversation allowed both partners to express themselves honestly.

Over time, mindfulness became a cornerstone of their relationship. They learned to anchor themselves in the present moment, appreciating the simple joys of time spent with their partner. Mindfulness activities like mindful breathing or going on nature walks helped them both not only relax, but also reconnect on a deeper level. The bond between them grew stronger, and they felt more secure and loved in each other's presence. They also set boundaries to protect their personal time and activities that were important to their individual growth.

Their journey served as a reminder that, even in the chaotic world of college life, mindfulness can provide the tools to enhance relationships and maintain a sense of presence, gratitude, and understanding, ultimately leading to a healthier and more enduring love. This does not only apply to romantic relationships, but also to our family ties, new friendships we make, and old friendships from before college.

Family

Embarking on the journey of college often means venturing into new territory, leaving behind the familiar embrace of family and childhood home. This transition can be marked by a whirlwind of emotions, from excitement and anticipation to apprehension and homesickness. Mindfulness provides a valuable anchor during this period of change. It encourages a non-judgmental observation of one's emotions, allowing you to acknowledge and validate your feelings without self-criticism. By recognizing and accepting these emotions, you can approach this new chapter with a greater sense of self-awareness and a deeper understanding of your own needs.

Chapter Five

Homesickness is a complex emotional experience that can affect college students profoundly. It's not just about missing the physical place of home, but also the sense of belonging, comfort, and the support system that home represents. The familiar sights, sounds, and routines of what you've known suddenly give way to a new, sometimes overwhelming environment on campus. You may long for the warmth of family interactions, the comfort of your own room, and the reassuring presence of familiar faces. The absence of family traditions and rituals can be hard too. These practices hold deep sentimental value, often rooted in shared history and cultural significance. Whether it's holiday celebrations, annual family trips, or even simple Sunday traditions, their absence can evoke a sense of loss and nostalgia.

Adapting to college life requires finding ways to recreate a sense of home in your new surroundings, whether through creating a cozy living space, maintaining regular communication with family, or establishing new comforting routines. It can also be helpful to create new traditions or find ways to incorporate elements of past rituals into your new environment, providing a sense of continuity and connection to family. Mindfulness can infuse new meaning by fully immersing you in the present moment and transforming the feelings of loss into an opportunity for creative expression and the formation of new meaningful rituals.

For international or out-of-state students, adapting to a new culture involves navigating a multitude of challenges. Language barriers, different social norms, and unfamiliar customs can lead to feelings of isolation and culture shock. As a student who has moved a considerable distance to a new culture, you may struggle with your sense of identity and belonging as you straddle your own cultural heritage with the demands of your new environment. Finding community through cultural clubs, engaging in cultural exchange programs, and seeking out spaces that celebrate diversity can be crucial for you in finding a sense of belonging and comfort in your new surroundings.

Despite the convenience of modern technology, you may still feel a sense of disconnection from your family. Factors like busy schedules, different time zones, and the demands of college life can make regular communication challenging. This sense of distance can lead to feelings of isolation and loneliness. It's important for you to proactively schedule regular check-ins with your family, finding a routine that works for both parties. Additionally, finding ways to stay connected beyond phone calls, such as sending care packages or planning virtual activities together, can help bridge the physical gap and maintain a strong sense of connection.

In the whirlwind of college life, it's crucial to remain mindful of the invaluable support and wisdom that family provides. Regular communication and involving them in your educational journey can enhance the experience for both you and your loved ones. Share your accomplishments, challenges, and aspirations with them, fostering a sense of togetherness and mutual understanding. Seek their advice and guidance, drawing from their life experiences and knowledge. Consider inviting them to special events or open houses at your college, allowing them to witness your growth and celebrate your achievements. By actively involving your family in your college education, you not only strengthen your support network but also maintain meaningful connections that enrich your overall experience.

Being away from home can increase concerns for the well-being of family members, especially if there are existing family issues or health concerns. You may be worrying about the health and happiness of your loved ones, and distance can exacerbate these feelings of helplessness. Establishing a communication routine and having open conversations about the well-being of family members can provide reassurance. Additionally, seeking support from campus resources or counseling services can help you navigate these concerns in a healthy and constructive way.

For some, navigating a strained or difficult relationship with family while in college can be an added layer of challenge. In such situations, it's essential to prioritize your own well-being and seek support where you can. Consider establishing healthy boundaries to protect your own emotional health, and seek out campus resources such as counseling services or support groups.

Building a chosen family or support network of friends and mentors can also provide a sense of belonging and emotional support. Engage in self-care practices that promote mental and emotional well-being, and explore activities or clubs on campus that align with your interests and values. Remember, you have the agency to shape your own path and define what 'family' means to you. Surround yourself with people who uplift and support you and know that you're not alone in this journey.

Old Friends

As college beckons, it brings with it a period of profound change. For many students, this includes a shift in social circles and a gradual drifting away from old friends. It's important to recognize that this evolution is a natural part of life's journey. As individuals grow and pursue different paths, interests may diverge, and priorities may shift. Mindfulness offers a valuable perspective during this transition. It encourages a non-judgmental awareness of these changes, allowing you to acknowledge that it is perfectly normal for friendships to come and go. By approaching this shift with mindfulness, you can navigate it with ease, honoring the memories and connections, while also embracing the potential for new relationships and experiences.

Leaving old friends behind can evoke a range of emotions, from nostalgia for shared experiences to a sense of loss for the familiarity and comfort they provided. Mindfulness invites you to approach these feelings with compassion and acceptance. Instead of suppressing or avoiding these emotions, mindfulness encourages you to sit with them, to acknowledge them without judgment. This process allows for a deeper understanding of oneself and the significance of these relationships in one's life.

Keeping cherished traditions alive is a powerful way to maintain the bond with old friends. Mindfulness enhances this experience by allowing you to fully immerse yourself in the moment. When you engage in these shared activities, practice mindfulness to savor every detail. Notice the sights, sounds, and emotions that accompany these traditions. This heightened awareness not only deepens your appreciation for the tradition but also strengthens the emotional connection between you and your friend. Additionally, mindfulness can help you adapt and evolve these traditions to fit your new circumstances, ensuring they remain relevant and meaningful in your college lives.

While the dynamics of friendships may change, it's important to recognize that the bonds forged with old friends hold a special place in one's heart. By embracing these feelings with mindfulness, you can find closure and appreciation for the impact these old friendships have had on your personal growth. Mindfulness prompts you to express gratitude for the time, experiences, and support shared with these friends. This might involve reaching out with a heartfelt message or simply taking a moment to reflect on the positive impact these individuals had on your life. By approaching this transition with a mindset of gratitude, you can ensure that the memories and lessons from these friendships continue to shape your journey, even as they embark on new paths.

Old friendships should be a source of encouragement as everyone embarks on their individual journeys. It's crucial to recognize and celebrate each other's achievements and personal growth. Mindfulness can amplify this support by fostering a deeper understanding of each other's unique paths. By practicing mindfulness, you can cultivate empathy and truly appreciate the significance of your friend's experiences. This heightened awareness allows you to offer more meaningful words of encouragement and advice, tailored to their specific situation. Moreover, mindfulness helps you remain present in your interactions, ensuring that you're fully engaged and available to support your friend during moments of triumph or challenge. Here are several ways old friends can support one another:

- Regular Check-Ins: Schedule video calls or phone chats to catch up on each other's lives and college experiences.

- Active Listening: Provide a non-judgmental ear

for each other to share triumphs, challenges, and personal developments.

- Encouragement: Celebrate each other's achievements and encourage the pursuit of new interests and academic endeavors.

- Respect for New Boundaries: Acknowledge and respect the new boundaries that may come with their changing lifestyles and priorities.

- Shared Experiences: If possible, visit each other's campuses to share in the unique experiences and cultures of different colleges.

- Advice and Feedback: Offer thoughtful advice and feedback on important decisions, valuing each other's insight as a trusted friend.

- Emotional Support: Be there for each other during tough times, providing comfort and reassurance when faced with the stresses of college life.

- Mindfulness Reminders: Encourage each other to stay grounded and mindful amid the hectic college environment.

- Networking: Help each other by sharing relevant contacts, like internships or academic resources, expanding each other's opportunities.

- Study Support: Be study buddies, even from afar, motivating each other to stay on track with coursework and exams.

- Space for Growth: Recognize and support each other's personal growth, understanding that people change and evolve, especially during college.

- Shared Goals: Set up shared goals or challenges, like reading the same book or taking similar online courses, to maintain a sense of camaraderie.

- Mutual Respect for Changes: Show appreciation for the new perspectives and changes that each brings to the friendship from their unique college experiences.

- Collaborative Projects: Engage in collaborative projects or activities that can be done remotely, like starting a podcast or a blog.

- Flexibility in Friendship: Stay flexible and adapt the friendship as needed, understanding that the frequency of communication might change, but the bond remains.

New Friends

In your first year or so of college, finding the right group of friends can be a transformative and enriching experience. It's important to seek out individuals who share your values, interests, and aspirations. Campus life is not just about classes and textbooks, you know? Attend club meetings, participate in campus events, and engage in activities that genuinely resonate with you. From joining clubs that may or may not align with your major, to participating in cultural or sports organizations, there are so many chances to explore passions and interests, while also fostering personal growth. It's an opportunity to expand horizons, form lasting connections, and develop skills beyond the classroom. Trust your instincts and seek out those who uplift and inspire you, fostering a supportive environment.

Quality over quantity is key; a smaller circle of genuine, like-minded friends can have a more profound impact on your college journey than a large group of acquaintances. Taking that step to get involved not only enriches your college journey but also helps you build a diverse and supportive community. It's through these experiences that you'll find camaraderie, discover new talents, and make memories that will shape your college years and beyond.

Ground rules aren't just for roommates. Set some for your campus involvement too. For example, decide how many events you'll check out each month or what clubs you'll join. It keeps you on track and prevents that FOMO from hitting too hard. And hey, be open to trying new stuff. College is like a buffet, right? Maybe you never thought you'd love painting, but guess what? Art club might just be your jam. So, keep an open mind, and who knows what cool experiences you'll stumble into.

Active Listening and Presence in Conversations

Making new friends in a college setting can be an exciting yet sometimes intimidating process. One of the cornerstones of mindful social interactions is the practice of active listening. This involves giving our full attention to the person we're conversing with, without distractions or the urge to formulate a response while they're speaking. By truly hearing and absorbing what others are saying, students can cultivate deeper connections and gain a better understanding of their peers. Additionally, mindfulness encourages students to be present in the conversation, rather than being preoccupied with past experiences or future concerns. This allows for more authentic and genuine interactions, laying the foundation for lasting friendships based on mutual respect and understanding. As Jon Kabat-Zinn wrote, "Learning how to listen and value the perspectives of others, especially if they are aversive in views, positions and methods, is an important part of healing divisions that can fester and turn toxic, as we see happening in so much of the world."

Mindfulness offers a valuable approach to these interactions, encouraging you to engage with an open mindset. This means letting go of assumptions or expectations about others and approaching each encounter with an open mind. By being fully present in the moment, you can actively listen and observe, allowing for more authentic and meaningful connections to form. This mindful approach to social interactions not only fosters a sense of acceptance and inclusivity but also creates a space where individuals feel heard and valued.

Inevitably, conflicts will arise as you and your friend(s) navigate the changes and challenges of college life. Open and honest communication is key to resolving disagreements and keeping small irritations from becoming points of conflict. Mindfulness plays a pivotal role here, as it encourages a non-judgmental approach to these conflicts. By practicing mindfulness, you can approach disagreements with a calm and clear mind, free from prior thoughts or biases. This allows for a more productive and constructive discussion, where both parties feel heard and understood. Mindfulness also helps you to empathize with your friend's perspective, even if it differs from your own, making it easier to resolve disputes and disagreements.

Dealing with Roommates

Sharing a living space with a roommate is a hallmark experience of college life. It's a dynamic that can shape not only the environment you come home to but also the interpersonal skills you develop along the way. Roommates can be really, really, really great or really, really, really awful! In either case, having a roommate offers you an opportunity to learn about compromise, communication, and the art of creating a harmonious living environment. Whether you're embarking on this journey for the first time or seeking ways to enhance an existing living situation, these tips can equip you with the tools and knowledge needed to foster a healthy, thriving relationship with your college roommate:

- Open Communication: Establish clear lines of communication from the beginning. Discuss expectations, boundaries, and preferences openly and respectfully.

- Set Ground Rules: Create basic rules for shared spaces, such as cleaning schedules, quiet hours, and personal space boundaries. This helps prevent potential conflicts.

- Respect Each Other's Space: It's important to spend time together, but also respect your roommate's need for personal time and space. Avoid going through their belongings or using their things without permission.

- Conflict Resolution: When conflicts arise, address them calmly and constructively. Use "I" statements to express your feelings and be open to hearing your roommate's perspective.

- Be Flexible and Compromise: Understand that compromise is essential. Flexibility in accommodating each other's preferences can lead to a more harmonious living arrangement.

- Maintain Personal Hygiene and Cleanliness: Keep shared spaces tidy and clean up after yourself. This helps create a comfortable living environment for everyone.

- Respect Diverse Backgrounds and Cultures: Be mindful of cultural differences and respect each other's traditions, beliefs, and practices.

- Establish Quiet Hours: Agree on designated times when noise levels should be kept low to ensure everyone has an opportunity for rest and study.

- Discuss Guests and Visitors: Communicate about having guests over and establish guidelines for how often and for how long guests are welcome.

- Share Expenses Fairly: If sharing expenses for shared items like groceries or household supplies, establish a system that is fair and transparent.

- Be Mindful of Personal Habits: Be considerate of habits that may affect your roommate, such as sleeping schedules, study habits, or personal routines.

- Celebrate Each Other's Achievements: Support and celebrate each other's successes, whether they're academic, personal, or extracurricular.

- Seek Mediation if Necessary: If conflicts persist and communication breaks down, consider seeking mediation or involving a resident advisor to help facilitate a resolution.

Remember, open communication and mutual respect are key to a successful roommate relationship. It's normal to encounter challenges, but addressing them with empathy and understanding can lead to a positive living experience for all involved.

Romance

Amidst this journey, romantic relationships often play a significant role, shaping the emotional landscape of students' lives. This section looks into the complicated realm of romantic relationships in the college environment. From the exhilarating highs of new connections to the complexities of long-distance relationships, navigating toxic dynamics, and the emotional terrain of breakups, we'll explore it all. These experiences are not only integral to the college narrative but are opportunities for self-discovery and growth.

In romantic relationships, mindfulness plays a pivotal role in fostering genuine and deep connections. At its core, mindfulness encourages present-moment awareness, which is particularly crucial in intimate partnerships. This means truly being present with one's partner, free from distractions or preoccupations. It involves active listening, where you fully engage with what your partner is saying, without formulating a response in your mind. By embracing this level of attentiveness, couples can establish a solid foundation of mutual understanding and respect. Mindful communication also extends to the expression of one's own feelings and needs, ensuring that both partners feel heard and valued in the relationship.

Setting Healthy Boundaries

Romantic relationships thrive when both individuals have a clear understanding of their own boundaries and respect those of their partner. Mindfulness supports this by encouraging self-awareness and introspection. It prompts you to reflect on your own needs, values, and limits, allowing you to communicate these effectively to your partner. Additionally, mindfulness helps foster a deep respect for each other's autonomy and individuality. It reminds couples that each person brings their own unique experiences and perspectives to the relationship. This mindful approach creates an environment where both partners feel free to express themselves and grow as individuals while still nurturing the bond they share.

Hook-Ups and Hard Nights

College life often brings new experiences, and for many, that includes the social dance of hooking up. While it's portrayed in movies as the peak of collegiate freedom, it's essential to handle these encounters with care and a good sense of humor. Think of hooking up as an elective course in personal connection—there's no set curriculum, and everyone's experience is subjective. It's not the end of the world; it's just another part of college life. The key is to ensure that every encounter is consensual, respectful, and-yes-safe. After all, safe sex is mindful sex. It's about being present in the moment, respecting your partner, and protecting the well-being of both parties involved.

Navigating the waters of casual relationships and encounters means students may sometimes face the infamous "walk of shame." Despite the term, there's no shame in having had a night of consensual fun. Society often sneaks in with whispers of judgment, but remember that how you feel about your choices is more important than what others might think. Then there's the aspect of self-forgiveness and not indulging in "slut-shaming" – especially towards yourself. College can be tough, riddled with high-pressure situations, and sometimes, you might end up making decisions that seem not so smart later on. But, it's these moments that often lead to stories you'll reminisce about and learn from. Whether it's a decision that makes you cringe or have a laugh, the key is to have fun, engage in mutual consent, and go easy on yourself. College is, after all, a time of learning and growth.

Who knows, your newfound love for mindfulness might even become a way of connecting with that hot barefooted hippie you always see at the library. Imagine finding common ground over a shared love for mindfulness and making a connection that's more than just physical. Hooking up can be a part of the journey, but it doesn't have to define it. So, stay safe, support your friends, and embrace the vibrant, occasionally chaotic, but always memorable college adventure.

Long Distance Relationships

Long-distance relationships (*dunnnn dunnnn*), often marked by physical separation, can be both emotionally rewarding and challenging. Unfortunately, high-school sweethearts won't always last. You may choose to navigate this new phase of your life with the belief that your connection with your partner is worth the extra effort despite the extra distance. The miles between partners can give rise to feelings of loneliness, longing, and even doubt. However, when approached with open hearts and a strong commitment, they can also foster deep emotional connections. It's also important to acknowledge that not every relationship separated by thousands of miles is going to last. Stings, right? But people grow apart, it's a part of life. It may hurt at first, being so comfortable with someone you've known for so long, then everything suddenly ends. It's important to acknowledge that maintaining a healthy long-distance relationship requires intentional effort from both parties. This includes regular communication, trust-building, setting goals to visit, maintaining independence, and finding creative ways to share experiences despite the physical distance.

Mindfulness, with its emphasis on present-moment awareness and non-judgmental acceptance, can be an invaluable tool for individuals in long-distance relationships. By cultivating mindfulness, partners can navigate the challenges with greater ease. Mindfulness encourages a focused awareness of both partner's own emotions and responses, which can help prevent misunderstandings and miscommunications. This practice also fosters a sense of patience and acceptance, enabling you to cope with the inevitable ups and downs of being apart. When practiced within a relationship, mindfulness can create a shared space of presence and emotional attunement, strengthening your relationship's bond.

There are specific mindfulness techniques that can be particularly beneficial for long-distance couples. Regular meditation, whether individually or together through virtual sessions, can help both partners find calm and center themselves. Engaging in mindfulness exercises like deep breathing or Body-Scans can also alleviate stress and promote emotional well-being. The Lovingkindness exercise, included in this chapter, is one way that long-distance couples can feel more connected. Additionally, setting clear intentions for communication and expressing gratitude for the moments shared, no matter how daunting, can infuse the relationship with a sense of purpose and appreciation. By integrating mindfulness into your long-distance journey, you have the opportunity to not only sustain their connection but also to grow individually and together, ultimately strengthening their relationship in profound and meaningful ways.

Toxic Relationships

College is a time of immense growth, self-discovery, and forging meaningful connections. It's a chapter in life where new experiences and relationships abound, shaping the course of one's future. While many of these connections are positive and enriching, there exists a harsh reality that is equally important to address: the presence of toxic relationships. These are interactions that can destroy one's emotional well-being, hinder personal development, and cast a shadow on what should be a time of optimism and exploration. During the college experience, toxic relationships can grow in various forms, from controlling romantic partnerships, to manipulative friendships, or even unhealthy dynamics within families. They can form from the very beginning of your new romance with an upperclassman, yet they're also possible to be revealed when high school romances turn into long-distance nightmares.

Understanding and navigating toxic relationships is essential for students seeking to thrive in their academic and personal pursuits. It requires recognizing the signs of toxicity, setting boundaries, and knowing when to seek support. This exploration dives into the intricacies of toxic relationships within the college environment, calling attention to the impact they can have on an individual's overall well-being. Through awareness and proactive measures, students can not only protect themselves from toxic influences but also foster an environment of positivity, respect, and personal growth as they embark on their educational journey.

Toxic Indicators, aka RED FLAGS

- Lack of Respect: In a healthy relationship, there is mutual respect for each other's boundaries, feelings, and autonomy. In a toxic relationship, one partner may consistently disrespect the other's boundaries, dismiss their feelings, or belittle them.

- Manipulation and Control: Toxic relationships often involve manipulation tactics such as guilt-tripping, gaslighting, or attempts to control the other person's actions or decisions.

- Constant Conflict and Negativity: While disagreements are a normal part of any relationship, in toxic relationships, conflicts are frequent, intense, and often leave one or both partners feeling drained, hurt, or unheard.

- Isolation from Support Systems: Toxic partners may seek to isolate their significant other from friends and family, making it difficult for them to seek outside perspectives or support.

- Lack of Trust and Accountability: In a healthy relationship, both partners take responsibility for their actions and are willing to apologize and make amends when necessary. In a toxic relationship, one partner may consistently deflect blame or refuse to acknowledge their harmful behavior.

Break-ups

Breakups can evoke a wide range of emotions, from sadness and grief to relief or even a sense of freedom. It's important to acknowledge that these feelings are valid, and each person navigates the aftermath of a breakup in their own way. For many, college is a time of personal exploration and growth, and sometimes this involves outgrowing or reassessing romantic partnerships. While breakups can be painful, they also present an opportunity for self-reflection and the chance to rediscover your own identity and aspirations.

It offers a way to process and manage the intense emotions that often accompany the end of a romantic relationship. By practicing mindfulness, you can create a space for self-compassion and acceptance, allowing yourself to honor your emotions without becoming overwhelmed by them. This practice encourages a gentle observation of thoughts and feelings, fostering a sense of inner calm and emotional stability during a sometimes challenging time. Moreover, mindfulness provides a foundation for making decisions with clarity and intention, helping you to move forward with a greater understanding of your own needs and aspirations.

By cultivating self-awareness through mindfulness, you can identify patterns, preferences, and values that will inform your future relationships. This practice also fosters a sense of resilience, enabling you to move forward with a renewed sense of purpose and a clearer vision of the kind of relationships that align with your authentic selves. Through mindfulness, the journey of healing from a college breakup transforms into an opportunity for growth, self-love, and the eventual pursuit of healthier, more fulfilling connections. Ultimately, relationships should feel like they energize you, not zap your energy. Sure, even the best relationships require work, that's true. But relationships – all of the good ones – should feel like they energize you. Full stop. When they never did or don't anymore, it's probably time to lean on mindfulness, and make some difficult, but healthy, decisions.

Exercise: Lovingkindness Meditation

Amidst lectures, assignments, and social endeavors, it's easy to overlook one of the most vital aspects of personal growth: the cultivation of inner compassion and kindness. Lovingkindness meditation, a practice steeped in ancient wisdom, offers a profound avenue to foster empathy, understanding, and genuine connection with oneself and others. It extends an invitation to delve into the depths of our hearts, where the seeds of compassion lie, waiting to be nurtured.

At its core, lovingkindness meditation is a transformative practice that seeks to cultivate boundless love and benevolence. It serves as a beacon of light, illuminating our capacity to foster warm, sincere relationships with those around us. In the context of college life, where forging new connections and nurturing existing ones is paramount, this practice takes on a profound relevance. It provides a powerful tool to navigate the complexities of friendships, romantic partnerships, and family dynamics with grace and authenticity.

This exercise offers insights into its techniques and the impact it can have on the fabric of relationships.

From enhancing self-compassion to fostering deeper connections with others, this practice holds the potential to enrich college life with kindness, empathy, and a genuine sense of community.

Step 1: Find a Quiet and Comfortable Space

- Choose a quiet place where you won't be disturbed.
- Sit or lie down in a comfortable position. You can use a cushion, chair, or lie on a yoga mat.

Step 2: Focus on Your Breath

- Close your eyes (if comfortable) and take a few deep breaths to center yourself.
- Allow your breathing to settle into a natural rhythm.
- Breath in through your nose and out through your mouth.

Step 3: Generate Lovingkindness for Yourself

Start by directing lovingkindness towards yourself. Repeat these or similar phrases silently or aloud:

"May I be happy."

"May I be healthy."

"May I be safe."

"May I live with ease."

Visualize yourself experiencing happiness, health, safety, and ease.

Step 4: Extend Lovingkindness to Others

Picture someone you care about deeply, such as a close friend or family member. Repeat the phrases for them:

"May [Name] be happy."

"May [Name] be healthy."

"May [Name] be safe."

"May [Name] live with ease."

Continue to extend these wishes to other loved ones.

Step 5: Expand to Neutral Individuals

Bring to mind someone you don't have strong feelings towards, like an acquaintance or a colleague. Offer them the same well-wishes:

"May [Name] be happy."

"May [Name] be healthy."

"May [Name] be safe."

"May [Name] live with ease."

Step 6: Include Difficult Individuals

Gradually, include people you may have had conflicts or difficulties with in the past or present. This is NOT a time for getting over trauma, so be gentle with who you focus on here. Once you've settled on a person, wish them well in the same way as before:

"May [Name] be happy."

"May [Name] be healthy."

"May [Name] be safe."

"May [Name] live with ease."

Step 7: Expand to All Beings

Imagine extending your lovingkindness to all beings around the world, without exception. You can say:

"May all beings be happy."

"May all beings be healthy."

"May all beings be safe."

"May all beings live with ease."

Step 8: End with Gratitude and Dedication

Take a moment to acknowledge the practice and the positive feelings you've generated.

Send gratitude to yourself for taking this time to cultivate lovingkindness.

Close your practice with an intention to carry this feeling of love and compassion into your day. As you open your eyes, don't struggle to move or get up fast, enjoy the sense of peace you have created and move when you are ready.

Remember, lovingkindness meditation is a skill that can be developed with practice. You can adjust the phrases to suit your own language and sentiments. Over time, this practice can lead to a greater sense of compassion, empathy, love for yourself, and others.

Reflection Questions

1. Consider a situation where you felt disconnected from your family while at college. How might mindfulness practices have helped you bridge that gap?

2. Have you considered how mindfulness can contribute to healthy boundaries and effective communication with roommates in a shared living space?

3. Have you identified any toxic relationship patterns in your life? How can mindfulness empower you to set healthy boundaries and prioritize your well-being?

4. How can you integrate the insights and practices shared in this chapter to cultivate more meaningful, balanced, and harmonious relationships in your college journey?

5. What steps can you take to apply mindfulness to difficult conversations and conflicts in your relationships, whether they are romantic, familial, or friendships?

178

Chapter Six

What's Your Zodiac?

Spirituality and religion are challenging obstacles to navigate, but with the proper approach and positive meditation practices, one can discover a world of new perspectives. Religion and spirituality are parts of a deeply personal journey, one that often involves self-discovery, exploration, and an open-minded approach. This chapter will guide you through an exploration of both from a neutral standpoint, aiming to cultivate your understanding while encouraging awareness. We will introduce a meditation practice in order to enhance self-discovery and gain an unbiased perspective on a wide array of religions that is a vital part of opening up to the fullness of what mindfulness (and college, for that matter) has to offer.

At the heart of many spiritual journeys is meditation. Meditation itself is not a religious practice, but rather an opportunity for exploration. It serves as a versatile tool, a gateway to a mindful approach, that can help you investigate religion and spirituality through a calm, introspective lens. Meditation transcends religious boundaries. It is a means of connecting with your inner self and exploring the depths of your consciousness. While it is true that meditation has been used in various religious traditions, it is not exclusive to any single belief system. In fact, it has been adopted by people of diverse backgrounds, from different cultures and spiritual inclinations, as a way to find inner peace, balance, and self-awareness. Learning about religion through a meditative lens offers a unique and insightful perspective. Meditation provides a calm and contemplative space where individuals can approach religious teachings with an open heart and a clear mind. By practicing mindfulness, one can engage with religious texts, rituals, and beliefs without preconceived judgments or biases. This approach allows for a deeper and more profound understanding of the spiritual and philosophical aspects of different religions, enabling individuals to connect with the core principles and values of each faith tradition. Through meditation, one can explore the common threads that run through various religions, such as compassion, love, and the quest for inner peace, and appreciate the rich tapestry of beliefs that contribute to the diverse spiritual landscape. In this way, meditation serves as a bridge for individuals to navigate the intricate world of religion, fostering respect, empathy, and a broader sense of spiritual awareness. As you embark on your spiritual journey, consider incorporating meditation into your daily routine. It can serve as a foundation for understanding and embracing various spiritual practices and beliefs. By cultivating a mindful approach, you'll be better equipped to explore the world of religion without preconceived biases, paving the way for a more profound and meaningful religious or spiritual life. This starts with being open to new ideas and experiences.

As you begin your college experience, you're not just stepping into a world of academic pursuits and extracurricular activities. You're also entering a vibrant, diverse community where individuals from various backgrounds come together to learn, grow, and share their unique perspectives. This dynamic combination of cultures, beliefs, and experiences is an invaluable part of your college life. Gaining a broad understanding of major religions is more than just acquiring knowledge; it's about embracing the beauty of diversity. It's important to remember that these differences, whether in the way one dresses, speaks, or prays, are not obstacles, but instead, opportunities for learning and growth.

College is a unique and transformative time in your life when you have the chance to build connections with a wide variety of people. These connections can be incredibly enriching, as they expose you to new perspectives, values, and ways of life. By engaging with individuals from diverse backgrounds, you'll not only broaden your horizons but also develop a deeper appreciation for the complexities of the human experience. One of the greatest benefits of interacting with a diverse community is the opportunity to appreciate diverse viewpoints. You'll have the chance to engage in meaningful conversations and discussions that challenge your existing beliefs and encourage you to see the world from different angles. These interactions foster intellectual growth and personal development, ultimately helping you become a more empathetic and open-minded individual. By welcoming and valuing all voices and perspectives, you create an environment that encourages meaningful dialogues and fosters mutual respect. Inclusivity doesn't mean conforming to a single set of beliefs; instead, it celebrates the richness of different cultures, faiths, and worldviews.

A fundamental aspect of spiritual exploration is the unbiased knowledge of a wide variety of religions. This knowledge is essential in making informed decisions about a person's own spirituality, as well as learning to non-judgmentally understand others' beliefs. It is important to approach this investigation with an open heart and a neutral perspective, allowing you to learn about the views and practices that have shaped the lives of countless individuals across the globe. In this section, we will provide a glimpse into several major religions that the reader will likely encounter during their college experience. These religions are not presented as the only options but serve as a starting point for your exploration. Understanding the key principles and practices of these religions will give you a deeper insight into the diversity of beliefs that shape our world.

Religions

In the heart of most world religions lies an invitation to introspection and contemplation that has echoed through the ages - a yearning for peace. This element of human experience, often including the practice of mindfulness, exceeds the bounds of any single tradition or dogma, revealing itself in the manifold expressions of the world's faiths. From the meditative disciplines of Buddhism, to the contemplative prayer of Christianity, to the reflective traditions of Islam's Sufism, to the introspective focus found in Hindu yoga, mindfulness has been a spiritual touchstone across divergent belief systems. Indeed, for those seeking to deepen their mindfulness practice, their own religious heritage might offer a wellspring of rich, contemplative practices, perfect for discovery and integration into their daily lives.

Understanding the religious context of mindfulness not only enriches one's personal practice but also fosters a broader cultural awareness. In an increasingly interconnected world, religious literacy – an understanding of diverse faiths and their practices – becomes a crucial skill, cultivating a space where multiple beliefs and customs can be approached with respect and curiosity. As students of mindfulness explore the depths of their own traditions, they gain a greater capacity for empathy and connection with others, appreciating spiritual expressions that contribute to the global human narrative. By embracing religious literacy, you do not only accumulate knowledge, but also develop mindfulness to honor the varied paths through which people seek meaning and connection.

Christianity

Christianity is one of the world's major religions, with over 2 billion followers worldwide. This is the most prevalent religion in the United States, with well over 50% of adults considering themselves Christian. It is rooted in the teachings and life of Jesus Christ, who is regarded as the Son of God. Christianity is characterized by faith in one God and the belief in salvation through Jesus Christ. Christian beliefs and practices vary widely, with denominations like Catholicism, Protestantism, and Eastern Orthodoxy offering unique perspectives and traditions. Central to Christianity is the Bible, a holy scripture that contains the Old and New Testaments. Practices often include attending church services, prayer, and living by a moral and ethical code. Despite the popularity of Christianity, it has recently been in decline. In the past, the Christian Churches of Europe actively participated in the colonization of areas across the globe. They had little regard for the inhabitants of these areas, solely focused on gaining wealth and land. These practices continue to have an impact on the reputation of the religion as a whole. For this reason, it is not uncommon for those in past colonized areas to possess a deep distrust of the Christian church. However, active attempts at reversing this damage are continuously made. It is important to acknowledge the Christian Church's mistakes of the past, as well as their current mission to remedy the damage they have left on Earth.

Christian mindfulness is often nurtured through prayer, meditation, and the reading of scripture. For instance, contemplative traditions within Christianity, such as the Centering Prayer, echo the silent communion with the divine, while the practice of Lectio Divina encourages a meditative approach to scripture, allowing believers to absorb the word of God deeply. The Spiritual Exercises of St. Ignatius of Loyola as well as writings from theologians like Thomas Merton offer structured reflections to foster discernment and spiritual insight for Christians all over the globe.

Islam

Islam is one of the world's most practiced religions with a global following of over 1.8 billion believers. It centers on the teachings of the Prophet Muhammad, which were revealed in the Quran, the holy book of Islam. Central to Islamic faith are the Five Pillars, which serve as the foundation of a Muslim's life. These include:

1. Shahada (Faith): The declaration of faith that affirms the oneness of God and the prophethood

of Muhammad.

2. Salat (Prayer): Muslims are required to pray five times a day, facing the Kaaba in Mecca.

3. Zakat (Almsgiving): An obligation to give to those in need, typically 2.5% of one's wealth annually.

4. Sawm (Fasting during Ramadan): During the month of Ramadan, Muslims fast from dawn to sunset as an act of worship and self-discipline.

5. Hajj (Pilgrimage to Mecca): Muslims who are physically and financially able are required to make the pilgrimage to Mecca at least once in their lifetime.

Islam places a strong emphasis on living in accordance with Islamic law, known as Sharia, which covers various aspects of life, including moral conduct, family law, and social justice. This legal framework ensures that Muslims lead lives that reflect the teachings of their faith. Islam is deeply rooted in community, and Muslims are encouraged to participate in acts of charity and service, reflecting their commitment to those less fortunate.

In Islam, mindfulness is integral to the daily prayers or Salah, which require a focused and intentional presence of mind. Beyond ritual prayer, Sufism, the mystical arm of Islam, engages in Dhikr, which involves chanting and meditation on the 99 names of Allah, allowing for a profound experience of remembrance and connection with the divine essence.

Buddhism

Buddhism, with over half a billion adherents world-wide, is a profound philosophy and religion founded by Siddhartha Gautama, known as the Buddha, or the "Awakened One." Buddhism emphasizes the Four Noble Truths, which are the foundational principles of the faith. These truths articulate the nature of suffering and the path to liberation from it. The Four Noble Truths are:

1. The Truth of Suffering: Recognizing the existence of suffering and its pervasive nature in human life.

2. The Truth of the Cause of Suffering: Identifying desire, attachment, and ignorance as the root causes of suffering.

3. The Truth of the End of Suffering: Understanding that suffering can be transcended and that there is a path to liberation.

4. The Truth of the Path to the End of Suffering: Outlining the Eightfold Path as the means to attain enlightenment and overcome suffering.

Central to Buddhist practice is meditation, which allows individuals to gain profound insights into the true nature of reality and of the self. However, it is important to recognize that meditating does not make a person Buddhist. Meditation is present in many faiths, as we have identified thus far. Buddhists seek to attain enlightenment and follow a code of ethics that includes principles of non-violence, mindfulness, compassion, and the cultivation of wisdom. Buddhism is a diverse faith with various traditions and schools, such as Theravada, Mahayana, and Zen Buddhism, each offering unique perspectives and practices.

A cornerstone of Buddhist practice is aiming to cultivate an awareness of the present moment. Through Vipassana meditation, meaning "to see things as they actually are," practitioners observe their thoughts and sensations without attachment, leading to a clearer understanding of the nature of suffering and the path to enlightenment. Mindfulness in Buddhism also extends to everyday activities, transforming them into opportunities for practice.

Hinduism

Hinduism, with approximately 1.2 billion followers, is one of the world's oldest and most complex belief systems. Central to Hinduism are concepts such as Dharma, Karma, and reincarnation. Hindus believe in a cycle of birth, death, and rebirth, with the ultimate goal of liberation from this cycle, known as Moksha, and union with the divine. Hindu practice includes a wide range of rituals, prayers, and meditation. The religion also places a strong emphasis on devotion to various deities, each representing different aspects of the divine. Hinduism's diversity is reflected in its many sacred texts, including the Vedas, Upanishads, and the Bhagavad Gita. These texts offer profound insights into the philosophical and spiritual dimensions of Hinduism.

Hinduism's rich tradition of mindfulness is perhaps best known through Yoga, which includes a variety of practices beyond physical postures, such as pranayama (breath control) and dhyana (meditation). These practices seek to quiet the mind and bring about a state of inner peace and unity with the divine consciousness, or Brahman.

Judaism

Judaism is one of the world's oldest monotheistic religions, with over 14 million followers worldwide. It is deeply rooted in the covenant between the Hebrew God and the people of Israel, as outlined in the Torah, the primary sacred text. Jewish practice includes observing the Sabbath, following a dietary code known as kosher, and celebrating festivals like Passover and Hanukkah. Judaism encompasses a rich tradition of prayer, study, and community life, with a strong emphasis on ethical conduct and social justice. This faith values community engagement and emphasizes the importance of tikkun olam, or repairing the world, through acts of kindness and social responsibility.

Chapter Six

Jewish mindfulness practices are deeply rooted in daily life and ritual. Mindfulness in Judaism is exemplified through the focused intentionality (kavanah) required during prayer and the study of the Torah. Additionally, the practice of hitbodedut entails a private, personal dialogue with God, offering a path to self-reflection and spiritual growth.

Sikhism

Sikhism is a monotheistic religion founded in the 15th century in the Punjab region of South Asia. It boasts a global following of over 30 million Sikhs. Sikhs believe in one God and the teachings of their Gurus, as recorded in the Guru Granth Sahib, the central religious scripture. Central to Sikhism is the concept of the community kitchen, or langar, where all are welcome to share a meal. This practice emphasizes the values of equality and service to others. Sikhs often wear the Five Ks, including the Kirpan (ceremonial sword) and Kara (steel bracelet), as symbols of their faith.

Mindfulness in Sikhism is cultivated through simran, the meditative remembrance of God's name, and through seva, or selfless service. These practices are meant to develop the individual's consciousness and to maintain a state of awareness and connection with the divine in daily life.

Chapter Six

Indigenous Religions

"Indigenous Religions" serves as a broad term for the diverse spiritual practices and beliefs of the world's original inhabitants, which are not traditionally included within the world religions. These traditions are as varied as the lands from which they arise, extending from the rich spiritual heritage of the San people of Africa to the varied indigenous cultures across the Americas, and even touching on ancient practices across Asia. Despite this diversity, a common thread in many indigenous belief systems is the conviction in a spirit world that transcends the visible, where ancestors and spiritual entities reside, influencing the material realm and guiding the living through dreams, visions, and shamanic journeys. Central to indigenous spiritualities is a profound reverence for nature, where the land itself is animate, sacred, and intricately linked to the identity and well-being of its people. Mountains, rivers, and forests are not merely resources or backdrops to human activity but are honored as vibrant entities, often interwoven with creation myths, moral laws, and life cycles. This deep ecological spirituality shapes the worldviews of indigenous peoples, prompting a life in rhythm with the natural order and a stewardship of the earth that is both spiritually and culturally important. Through rituals, ceremonies, and the living oral tradition, these beliefs and practices foster cultural identity amidst the changing landscapes of the modern world.

Mindfulness, in indigenous religious traditions, is often expressed through a deep attention to nature and the cycles of life. Rituals, ceremonies, and the oral tradition of storytelling are combined with attentiveness to the present and a profound respect for the interconnectedness of all beings, reflecting a harmonious relationship with the Earth and its inhabitants.

Spirituality

The information on religion provided above is not meant to compel you to adopt a specific faith. Instead, it is a guide to help you discover where you belong on the broad spectrum of spiritual practices or even create your unique path to spiritual fulfillment.

Spirituality, as a concept, has gained traction in recent decades as a way to describe people who may still believe in God or a cosmic force for good in the universe, but who can't get past all the traditions or tragedies that have come with religions in history. There's even a term for these folks, "Spiritual but Not Religious," and their numbers grow every single year, especially on college campuses, as well as the creation of spirituality-focused content on social media.

Chapter Six

Spirituality is a deeply personal and evolving journey, where college is a perfect opportunity for exploration. As you embrace the diversity of beliefs and practices that college offers, you will find your spiritual journey to be enriched, your heart to be more open, and your mind to be more inquisitive. This is not just about academic growth; it's about becoming a more compassionate and well-rounded individual who is ready to embrace the beautiful complexities of the world.

In this section, you'll discover that true spiritual fulfillment doesn't come from rigid beliefs or doctrines but from the connections you build, the perspectives you understand, and the compassion you carry with you. It's a path that leads to a profound sense of interconnectedness and an appreciation for the tapestry of human experience. Your college years are your opportunity to start walking that path, hand in hand with a diverse community that welcomes you as you are and encourages you to be your best self.

Just as there's a vast variety of religions, there is a multitude of spiritual practices that people passionately believe. These practices offer unique avenues for self-discovery, personal growth, and well-being. It's important to understand these beliefs, whether you find yourself vigorously believing in them or only slightly interested, in order to comprehend and sympathize with the experiences of others. Your college experience will introduce you to a diverse range of beliefs and practices and understanding them is an essential aspect of your spiritual journey. Here's a list of some of the practices and activities that are today often associated with spirituality:

- Meditation: This one's no surprise. Meditation is one of the cornerstones of "spirituality" and is an important foundation in many spiritual traditions for cultivating inner peace and insight.

- Prayer: A form of communication with a deity or spirit, prayer is used in almost every spiritual tradition to seek comfort, make requests, or express gratitude, often with profound personal and communal significance.

- Yoga: Originating in ancient India, yoga encompasses a range of physical, mental, and spiritual practices aimed at achieving unity between the self and the divine or universal consciousness.

- Sacred Rituals: There are prescribed ceremonies or actions carried out with spiritual intent, often in accordance with the traditions of a community or culture, such as baptisms in Christianity or puja in Hinduism.

- Fasting: Abstaining from food or drink for a period of time as a means of purification, self-discipline, or communion with the divine, fasting is present in many spiritual paths as a practice of surrender and dedication.

- Chanting and Mantras: The repetitive utterance of sounds, words, or phrases, often considered sacred, as a form of spiritual devotion, meditation, or to induce an altered state of consciousness.

- Reading and Reflection on Sacred Texts: Engaging with spiritual scriptures, such as the Bible, Qur'an, Bhagavad Gita, etc., provides insights into the divine, moral guidance, and reflection for personal growth.

- Séance: A séance is a gathering where individuals seek to communicate with spirits, particularly the spirits of the dead. This is often facilitated by a medium, someone who claims to have the ability to contact and communicate with the spiritual realm. Séances are typically conducted with the intention of gaining insight from the beyond or finding closure with past loved ones.

- Tarot: Tarot involves the use of a deck of cards, each with symbolic imagery and meaning, for divination or to gain insight into complex situations and the subconscious. It's a reflective practice that can help articulate the present moment and provide guidance for future decisions, regarded by many as a tool for self-discovery and personal growth.

- Alternative Healing: This is a broad category that includes various non-traditional health practices believed to heal not just the body but also the soul. Examples include crystal healing, sound therapy, and aromatherapy. Practitioners often view health and wellness as a holistic integration of the physical, emotional, and spiritual components of a person.

- Pilgrimage: A journey to a sacred place or shrine of importance to a person's beliefs and faith. Pilgrimages are often acts of devotion and searching for deeper meaning or enlightenment.

- Nature Communion: Finding spiritual connection and reflection through the natural world, recognizing the sacred in the living ecosystem, and seeing nature as a source of inspiration and revelation.

- Service and Charity: Acts of altruism and volunteer work can be spiritual practices, reflecting the belief in the interconnectedness of all life and the importance of kindness and compassion.

- Retreats: Participating in retreats offers a time of seclusion for meditation, prayer, and self-reflection, often away from the distractions of everyday life, to deepen one's spiritual connection.

- Energy Healing: Modalities such as Reiki, qigong, and others, are based on the concept of manipulating the energy fields around the body to promote healing and spiritual well-being.

- Contemplative Arts: Practices like calligraphy,

sacred dance, or icon painting that are performed with a meditative mindset, aiming to express and experience the spiritual.

• Study of Philosophy and Metaphysics: Engaging with philosophical ideas and existential questions can be a spiritual practice for those who seek understanding about the nature of reality and the universe from a spiritual perspective.

As you might notice, this list is kind of "all over the place," demonstrating that we don't really have a firm idea of what "Spirituality" even means. Each of these modalities can serve as a pathway to the individual's understanding of spirituality, providing a means to explore and express their intrinsic connection to the larger mysteries of existence. The concept is a moving target, still gaining a definition as people make sense of their lives and find mindful value in countless ways outside of (and sometimes, within) traditional religions. We'll now spend a little time focusing on a few spiritual practices growing in popularity on college campuses, astrology, crystal healing, and aromatherapy.

Astrology

Astrology is a popular system that uses a person's birth date and time to project their personality and life path.

Your astrology chart, often referred to as your "natal chart," is a personalized map of the celestial bodies at the moment of your birth. It contains insights into your personality traits, strengths, weaknesses, and potential life path. Astrology is an intriguing and sometimes polarizing subject. While some people wholeheartedly embrace astrology as a guiding force in their lives, others view it with skepticism, but the greatest majority lie in the middle of the spectrum. It is possible to only partially commit to the study of astrology.

An astrology chart, or natal chart, is a complex representation of the positions of the planets and other celestial bodies at the exact time and place of your birth. The four most notable parts of the natal chart are planets, zodiac signs, houses, and aspects. Each planet in the solar system has a specific significance in astrology. For instance, Mercury is associated with communication and learning, while Mars is linked to energy and passion. Then, the twelve zodiac signs represent distinct personality traits and characteristics. For example, Aries is associated with courage and assertiveness, while Taurus is linked to stability and sensuality. Houses are another division of the chart. The twelve segments of the astrology chart are each associated with different life areas. For instance, the first house is linked to the self, while the seventh house pertains to relationships. Finally, aspects are the relation of different areas within the chart. They are specific angles formed between the planets, revealing different energies and potential challenges. For instance, a conjunction represents intense energy, while a square indicates tension.

To explore astrology, you can begin by generating your own natal chart. There are numerous online tools and websites that can help you create your chart for free. Once you have your chart, you can explore it to gain insights into your personality, strengths, and potential challenges. Interpreting your natal chart can be a complex process, and many individuals seek the guidance of professional astrologers for a more comprehensive analysis. However, there are also many books and online resources available that provide guidance on how to interpret your chart. It's essential to note that astrology has its share of critics who view it as a pseudoscience with no empirical basis. Skeptics argue that the personality traits attributed to specific zodiac signs are overly generalized and do not account for the complexity of individual personalities. As you explore astrology, it's important to maintain a balanced perspective and decide for yourself whether it resonates with your journey of self-discovery. While astrology may not align with your beliefs, learning about it can offer insights into the perspectives and practices of others. By understanding astrology, you can engage in meaningful conversations and develop empathy for those who embrace it as a valuable tool for self-reflection.

Crystals & Aromatherapy

Crystal healing is a custom that involves using specific crystals to address physical, emotional, and spiritual concerns. Crystals have been used for centuries for their believed healing properties. Different crystals are thought to have distinct properties, such as promoting healing, protection, or balance. Crystal healing is not a replacement for medical treatment but rather an approach that complements overall well-being. Here are some commonly used crystals and their associated properties:

- Amethyst: Known for promoting spiritual growth and emotional balance.

- Rose Quartz: Believed to enhance love and compassion.

- Citrine: Associated with abundance and positive energy.

- Clear Quartz: Often used for clarity and amplifying intentions.

Crystal healing is based on the idea that each crystal has a unique vibrational frequency and energy. These energies can interact with the body's energy centers, or chakras, to promote balance and healing. Chakra meditation, originating from Hindu traditions, focuses on aligning and balancing the body's energy centers. The practice involves meditating on each of the seven chakras to unlock and enhance different aspects of your physical and spiritual well-being.

While scientific evidence on crystal healing is limited, many individuals find these practices to be soothing and beneficial. The way you use crystals in your spiritual journey is highly personal. Some people carry specific crystals with them, wear crystal jewelry, or use them during meditation. Others place crystals in their living spaces to enhance the overall atmosphere and energy. Like Astrology, there are many online and printed resources that further dive into the specifics. As you explore crystal healing, remember that it's not a one-size-fits-all approach. The key is to find the crystals that resonate with you and enhance your well-being. The best way to determine this is to experiment. Numerous online retailers sell minerals specifically for crystal healing, though it is generally more rewarding to search for crystals in nature. Hunting for crystals is a perfect opportunity to practice walking meditation, cultivating mindfulness and discovering spirituality. A guide to successfully implementing walking meditation is provided at the conclusion of this chapter.

Essential oils are extracts from plants, trees, and other natural sources that are often used for what's called "Aromatherapy," the mindful practice of finding peace and calmness through your sense of smell. They are believed to have therapeutic properties and are used for various purposes, including relaxation, stress relief, pain-management, as well as ingredients in perfumes and cosmetics. The practice of using essential oils for healing purposes is what makes up Aromatherapy, and it involves inhaling the scents of these oils or applying them topically. Here are a few essential oils and their potential benefits:

- Lavender: Known for its calming and stress-relief properties. It can promote relaxation and help alleviate anxiety and sleep issues.

- Peppermint: Often used to enhance focus and mental clarity. The invigorating scent of peppermint can help with alertness and concentration.

- Eucalyptus: Believed to aid in respiratory health and provide a sense of invigoration. It can be particularly helpful during cold and flu season.

- Lemon: Used to uplift moods and enhance overall wellness. Lemon essential oil is often associated with a fresh and clean scent.

Aromatherapy has a rich history that goes back centuries. Ancient civilizations, including the Egyptians, Greeks, and Romans, recognized the healing properties of aromatic plants. The Egyptians used essential oils in embalming and cosmetics, while the Greeks and Romans used them for their medicinal benefits.

Chapter Six

Essential oils are extracted from different parts of plants through methods such as distillation and cold-pressing. The process of extraction ensures that the beneficial properties of the plant are preserved in concentrated form. This strong concentration means oils must be diluted with a carrier oil if they are to be applied to the skin. A common dilution ratio is 3-5 drops of essential oil per teaspoon of carrier oil. Each bottle will have instructions as to the proper use and healing effects. A common method of employing essential oils in the home is a diffuser. Diffusers are used to disperse the aromatic molecules of essential oils into the air, creating a pleasant atmosphere and promoting well-being. Besides the healing benefits of diffusers, they also function as a natural alternative to chemical air fresheners. Aromatherapy is often used in combination with massage as a complementary therapy for various health and wellness concerns. It can also be a powerful tool for managing stress and promoting relaxation. Using essential oils can be a delightful and soothing addition to your daily routine. You can explore these scents through diffusers, topical application, or by adding a few drops to a relaxing bath. Conveniently, they are affordable and easy to obtain. Almost all department stores stock a selection of essential oils. Whether you are looking for stress relief, enhanced focus, or a boost in overall well-being, essential oils offer a wide range of options to support your journey of self-discovery.

In the realm of spirituality, there are countless avenues of exploration, from astrology to crystal healing and essential oils. These practices are deeply personal, and you have the freedom to choose what resonates with your circumstance. Each of these paths offers unique opportunities for self-discovery, personal growth, and connection with others. If none of the beliefs listed felt intriguing, do not worry. The internet is a gateway to exploration, and there are numerous other ways to be spiritually involved. Likewise, if this involvement feels forced, remember it is not necessary that you experience a belief. The crucial aspect of this learning is to understand how to be aware of spiritual possibility and utilize mindfulness to determine your personal beliefs. As you explore these practices and others, you will find that they can provide comfort, support, and guidance on your path of self-discovery.

Remember that the journey is not about rigid beliefs or doctrines. Instead, it's about the connections you build, the perspectives you understand, and the compassion you build. By embracing diversity and practicing inclusivity, you'll embark on a path that leads to a strong sense of interconnectedness and an appreciation for the intricacies of the human experience. Your college years offer the perfect opportunity to begin this enriching journey, along with a diverse community that welcomes and encourages you to be your best self. Embrace diversity, nurture inclusivity, and approach spirituality with an open heart and inquisitive mind. Your spiritual journey is your own, and it's one that offers profound insights, personal growth, and a deeper connection to the world around you.

Maria's Story

During their college years, students often navigate a period of exploration, each tackling this phase in unique ways. While some find peace in mindfulness and meditation, others may find themselves without many strategies to cope with life's stressors. Maria's exploration into the world of spirituality became a defining feature of her university days.

Maria arrived on campus with the typical freshman eager: excited to learn, make friends, and uncover her identity. She encountered many cultures and beliefs that were starkly different from her small-town background. Raised in a mainly Christian household, she was now amidst a melting pot of faiths and practices, which initially left her feeling out of place.

Intrigued by her peers' diverse spiritual expressions, Maria took a step back and observed. Her roommate was a practitioner of Buddhism, finding peace in the daily rhythms of meditation. Her best friend, coming from far shores, adhered to the Hindu faith with a passion that was both fascinating and alien to Maria. And then there was her study partner in Shakespearean Literature, an individual whose passion for astrology often steered their discussions to the alignment of stars and planets.

Astrology, a concept once foreign to Maria, slowly started to grab her interest. It wasn't just about knowing your sun sign; it was about understanding how celestial movements could influence personal growth and character traits. She found herself more and more involved, checking her birth chart and finding comfort in the personality descriptors that seemed to align with her own self-image. Astrology didn't demand belief; it offered a framework for understanding oneself and others, bridging the gap between Maria and her new college acquaintances.

Maria's initial academic confidence wavered as finals approached, especially with the looming challenge of her Calculus exam. Her studies seemed insufficient, her preparation lacking. It was during a conversation, filled with her concerns, that her roommate introduced her to the practice of meditation. The suggestion led Maria to a local meditation circle, which was a diverse group of individuals who found commonality in seeking inner peace. The calming practice eased her anxiety, armed her with confidence, and saw her through to secure an A- on her daunting exam.

Returning to campus after the winter break, Maria didn't hesitate to dive back into the meditation group. Each session, she listened intently to stories that expanded her horizon, teaching her that there were numerous ways to reach spiritual enlightenment. The group, with its eclectic mix of backgrounds, became a beacon of unity and acceptance for Maria.

Maria's spiritual quest was not defined by the confines of a single doctrine. Rather, it was a colorful blend of practices that resonated with her spirit. From her roommate's Buddhist teachings, to the zodiac charts that now adorned her study space, her spiritual palate expanded in depth and breadth. Her journey underscores that spirituality is an intimate exploration, one that can be navigated during the transformative college years. It's a personal passage where exploration, understanding, and acceptance combine, allowing you to learn not only from textbooks but from the richness of the college experience and wisdom.

Exercise: Walking Meditation

Maria's journey was greatly improved by her wise decision to explore meditation. Meditation and mindfulness are essential tools in the drawer of a confused student. They allow the mind freedom of thought impossible when preoccupied and stressed with the rigors of school. One such practice is walking meditation, which allows connection between the mind and the body while in motion. This practice can be particularly appealing for individuals who find it challenging to sit still for extended periods. Physical activity is always a positive coping strategy, but mindfulness allows one to structure their experience. Walking with no purpose can mindfully be shaped into a meditative expedition. It is also a wonderful way to harmonize the mind, body, and spirit with the present circumstances.

Step 1: Find a Quiet Space

Choose a location where you can walk peacefully without distractions. It could be a garden, a park, or simply a quiet path.

Step 2: Stand Still

Begin by standing still and taking a few deep breaths. Allow yourself to fully arrive in the present moment. Be still and bring your breath in through your nose, and exhale slowly through your mouth. Do this with intention several times. What's happening around you? Is it windy? Cold? Warm?

Step 3: Mindful Steps

Start walking slowly, focusing on each step. Pay attention to the sensation of lifting your foot, moving it forward, and placing it down. Be aware of the ground beneath your feet.

Step 4: Breathing Awareness

Coordinate your breath with your steps. Take two steps and align your breathing with the steps. For some of you, this may mean three to four steps per breath. For others, it might only be two steps per breath. Check in with the rhythm of your body. This synchronizes your movements and breath, creating a sense of harmony.

Step 5: Stay Present

As you walk, check in with your thoughts and emotions. Pay attention to the kind of thoughts and feelings you are experiencing, note them, and let them pass you by, returning your awareness back to breathing and stepping.

Step 6: Observing Nature

If you're walking outdoors, take time to observe nature. Notice the colors, shapes, and sounds around you. If you're indoors, perhaps train your attention to the mechanics of your body. How are your joints and muscles working to create the opportunity of walking. This can enhance your connection with the environment and spirituality.

Step 7: Mantras or Affirmations

You can incorporate mantras or affirmations into your walking meditation. For example, you might silently say, "I am at peace" with each step. This can deepen your spiritual connection.

Step 8: Turn Around

When you reach the end of your walking path, pause for a moment and turn around mindfully. If you are on a short path, perhaps make an additional lap. If you are on a longer trail or sidewalk, perhaps quickly assess how far you plan to walk.

Step 9: The Last Step

As you conclude your walking meditation, stand still once again. Take a few moments to acknowledge the practice and express gratitude for the experience.

A walking meditation is a beautiful way to explore your spirituality through movement and mindfulness. It allows you to find inner peace, reduce stress, and deepen your connection with the present moment. You can incorporate walking meditation into your daily routine, whether it's a short stroll during a break or a longer meditative hike in nature. In your journey of self-discovery, remember that there is no one-size-fits-all approach to spirituality. It's a personal exploration that can take many forms, from seated meditation to walking meditation, and even a blend of various practices. As you embrace your mindfulness practice, you'll find your unique path to inner peace and spiritual fulfillment.

Reflection Questions

1. How can the practice of mindfulness enhance our understanding and respect for the diverse spiritual traditions we encounter, as exemplified by Maria's exposure to various beliefs at her college?

2. In what ways does mindfulness serve as a common thread among different religious practices, and how can individuals leverage this shared aspect to foster interfaith dialogue and personal spiritual growth?

3. Reflect on the role of mindfulness in aiding personal discovery and peace of mind, as seen in Maria's journey. How can adopting mindfulness practices contribute to one's spiritual development amidst the pressures of academic life?

4. Considering the various modalities of spirituality, such as meditation, prayer, or contemplative walks in nature, how does mindfulness connect and differ across these practices, and what does that tell us about the universal pursuit of inner peace?

5. Reflect for a moment on your current schedule? When could you work in a Walking Meditation? Pull out your phone, look at your calendar, and pick a time. This is the current you deciding to do something good for your future you. Celebrate it now and work to experience gratitude when the day and time comes for your Walking Meditation.

Chapter Seven

Levelin' Up

"Congratulations, you've graduated!" The cheers and applause that filled the auditorium on that fateful day were a culmination of years of hard work and dedication. You will likely be excited, but as the celebrations fade, the weight of the future might loom like a heavy cloud. Life after college may start to present itself as a labyrinth of challenges and uncertainties.

Graduating from college is a transformative milestone. It signifies the conclusion of one chapter and the commencement of another, an adventure that can be both exhilarating and daunting. For recent graduates, this time is marked with changes and challenges, such as finding a job, achieving financial stability, and launching into a life of your own making. The excitement of newfound freedom is mixed with some uncertainty, and the path forward may be unclear. Yet, this very transition is where mindfulness can be embraced as your guiding star.

In this chapter, we will look at how mindfulness can be a beacon of light in the transition from college to post-college life. You'll discover how it can assist you in managing stress, anxiety, and uncertainty, particularly during the job search process and beyond. Together, we will explore how mindfulness can empower you to stay calm, focused, and resilient.

Mindfulness is not a distant concept or an obscure practice reserved for gurus. As you should know by now, it's a tangible and valuable tool that can be harnessed by anyone – including you. It involves immersing yourself fully in the present moment, unburdened by judgment or preconceived notions. Instead of letting your mind wander to the past or future, mindfulness encourages you to embrace the "here and now." The ability to be fully present is a skill that can be honed over time, and its relevance in the post-college phase is undeniable. By paying attention to the present moment, you can better manage stress, anxiety, and uncertainty as you navigate the challenges that come your way.

After Graduation

The post-college phase often begins in the challenging quest for employment, a journey with the pressure to secure a job, the looming possibility of rejection, and the ever-present anxieties that can quickly become overwhelming. It is here that mindfulness emerges as a steady hand amid the challenging times, a source of support that allows you to maintain composure. What follows in this section are some specific mindfulness techniques that can seamlessly blend into your daily job search routine. These are more than just strategies; they are your guiding stars as you navigate the unpredictable times of the job market. Among these techniques, mindful breathing exercises and mindfulness for public speaking stand out as powerful tools that empower you to approach the job search journey with clarity and composure.

Mindful Breathing

Mindful breathing is a fundamental practice in the art of stress management. We explored it in several places already, such as the Introduction and in Chapter Three when we described the Box Breathing technique, but it's worth drilling down on one last time. Breathing is a deceptively simple yet profoundly effective technique that can serve as your anchor when the world around you appears to be in chaos. This practice requires nothing more than a few moments of your time, yet its impact is immeasurable.

Imagine this: you find a quiet moment, and with intention, you take a deep breath. Inhale, and you can feel the air filling your lungs, oxygenating your body. As you exhale, you release the tension and anxiety that may have accumulated. This act of conscious breathing is not just a physical act; it's a mental and emotional one as well. It brings you back to the present moment, grounding you amidst the whirlwind of uncertainties.

As you engage in mindful breathing, you become the eye of the storm, unaffected by the chaos swirling around you. It's in this center of composure that you make the most informed decisions, project confidence during interviews, and handle inevitable rejections with ease. Mindful breathing makes the job search not just a quest for employment, but a profound personal development journey. Through this practice you will not just grow professionally, but also as a person, anchored in composure and grace.

Coping with Rejection Anxiety

Rejection is an inevitable part of life after college. Whether it's a job application that receives a polite "No," or an interview that doesn't yield the desired outcome, coping with rejection sensitivity can be challenging. In this chapter, we will explore the tools that mindfulness techniques provide for managing anxiety and building resilience.

Through practices that promote self-compassion and a reframing of setbacks as opportunities for growth, you will uncover strategies for maintaining your self-esteem and facing rejection. Mindfulness will empower you to persevere through these setbacks without losing sight of your worth and potential.

One of the mindfulness techniques that can be particularly helpful in dealing with rejection sensitivity is self-compassion. It involves treating yourself with the same kindness, care, and understanding that you would offer to a close friend. Instead of harshly criticizing yourself for perceived shortcomings or mistakes, you approach yourself with warmth and empathy. This practice can help you get through the blows of rejection more gracefully and maintain your self-esteem.

Time Management

With the transition to post-college life comes a shifting landscape of responsibilities and an increased demand for effective time management. Juggling the intricacies of work, personal life, and self-care can feel overwhelming. However, mindfulness serves as an invaluable tool in this domain, allowing you to take advantage of the power of the present moment to enhance your time management skills.

Mindful time management techniques, including the Pomodoro technique and Time-Blocking, offer pathways to heightened productivity and reduced stress. These strategies enable you to focus more intently on the task at hand and lessen distractions.

The Pomodoro technique encourages the fragmentation of work into short, focused intervals, typically 25 minutes in length, followed by a brief rest. This method aligns seamlessly with mindfulness principles, as it encourages you to immerse yourself fully in the task at hand. It also aids in maintaining your work-life balance by providing designated periods for rest and rejuvenation.

Time-blocking involves scheduling specific blocks of time for various activities, ensuring that you allocate dedicated time for work, personal growth, hobbies, and relaxation. Mindfulness comes into play by allowing you to be present during each designated block, enhancing your productivity and overall well-being.

Communication

Effective communication is the cornerstone of building meaningful relationships in the post-college world. Mindfulness stands as a powerful ally in this endeavor, offering you an enhanced ability to listen actively and empathize with others.

As you navigate through professional and personal relationships, mindfulness can significantly improve your communication skills. The art of mindful listening involves giving your full attention to what others are saying without judgment. This empathetic approach to communication not only forms a deeper connection with others but also reduces the likelihood of misunderstandings and conflicts.

Mindful speaking complements mindful listening. It encourages you to express your thoughts and feelings with a heightened sense of self-awareness. For instance, mindful public speaking involves focusing on the present moment, calmly acknowledging and accepting one's feelings and thoughts. This practice encourages speakers to engage with their audience authentically, fostering a connection rooted in genuine expression and active listening. By embracing mindfulness, speakers can effectively manage anxiety and deliver their message with clarity and confidence. By speaking mindfully, you can convey your messages clearly and effectively while remaining attuned to the impact of your words on others.

In a world where the power of effective communication is essential, the techniques introduced in this chapter serve as invaluable tools for building positive and meaningful relationships with colleagues, friends, and potential mentors. Through mindfulness, your communication becomes a bridge that connects you with others on a deeper level.

Conflict Resolution

Conflicts, as you are undoubtedly aware, are an inescapable event of both your personal and professional life. They tend to emerge when diverse perspectives, goals, and expectations intersect. In such moments of tension, the tools of mindfulness emerge as valuable assets. Applied to the intricate art of conflict resolution, mindfulness offers an effective means to navigate these inevitable clashes with ease and clarity.

Mindfulness empowers you with a set of inner tools, such as mental resilience, emotional intelligence, and self-awareness, that are instrumental when it comes to addressing conflicts in a constructive manner. It's about being present in the moment, fostering a deeper understanding of yourself and those around you, and embracing an open-minded, non-judgmental approach to resolve differences. These attributes provide you with the ability to explore alternatives, bridge gaps, and reach solutions that honor the perspectives of all involved stakeholders.

Chapter Seven

This chapter extends the discussion into specific strategies tailored to harness the power of mindfulness for conflict resolution. At its core, these strategies revolve around keeping your composure, remaining focused, and maintaining objectivity during challenging conversations. These are actionable techniques that can be employed when conflicts arise, serving to transform potentially volatile encounters into opportunities for growth.

Through mindfulness, you can remain focused on the present moment and prevent your mind from wandering into past grievances or future concerns. You can also approach disputes with a clear and unclouded perspective. Maintaining objectivity means that you can assess situations without bias by embracing different viewpoints and reaching fair resolutions that consider the interests and well-being of all people or groups involved.

The practical application of these techniques can lead to more harmonious relationships, in either your professional endeavors or personal interactions. They foster better collaboration with colleagues and peers, ensuring that you can resolve disputes while preserving the integrity of your connections. The ultimate aim of these strategies is not only to suppress or eliminate conflicts, but to transform them into stepping stones for personal and collective growth. This will reinforce bonds and create a more supportive and constructive environment for all involved.

Goal Setting

As you set your sights on your post-college ambitions, mindfulness can be a transformative force in your goal-setting process. It empowers you to set realistic and meaningful goals, break them down into manageable steps, and remain resolutely focused on achieving them.

Mindfulness and goal setting are a natural pairing. By cultivating mindfulness, you become more attuned to your inner desires and aspirations. This heightened self-awareness enables you to establish goals that genuinely resonate with your values, passions, and life vision.

Mindfulness also encourages you to break these overarching goals into smaller, achievable steps. By creating a roadmap of incremental milestones, you set yourself up for a higher likelihood of success. This mindful approach to goal setting promotes the growth of patience and perseverance, allowing you to stay resolute and strong in your pursuit of professional and personal fulfillment.

Building Resilience

Resilience, the unwavering spirit that empowers you to bounce back from life's inevitable setbacks, is a vital trait as you navigate life beyond college. The post-academic journey, fraught with its distinct set of trials, requires a profound inner strength, and mindfulness can be the key to cultivating this strength.

The practice of gratitude journaling offers more than just cherishing moments of abundance; it enables you to achieve a state of strong resilience. By faithfully recording your daily blessings, no matter how seemingly inconsequential, you develop a profound sense of appreciation. But this appreciation goes beyond simple thankfulness. It instills within you an unbreakable belief in your own strength. Each reflection on your achievements serves as a reminder of how you've successfully navigated past obstacles. This retrospective wisdom strengthens you, preparing you for future challenges with the assured knowledge that setbacks are just fleeting moments in the greater story of your life. You become unbothered by life's uncertainties, approaching them with a calmness that nothing can disturb.

Visualization, as another powerful mindfulness tool, encourages you to imagine yourself facing adversity with grace, determination, and above all, patience. By mentally rehearsing your response to challenges, you strengthen your capacity to rebound from setbacks with greater control. Visualization empowers you to transform challenges into opportunities for growth, approaching them with a graceful demeanor. Exercises like visualization and journaling allow you to navigate the unpredictable waters of life with strong composure, seeing setbacks as momentary learning curves on your path towards success.

The power of mindfulness, gratitude journaling, and visualization exercises makes you not just resilient but cool under pressure. You develop an enduring mindset, unaffected by life's trials, and balanced to use them to your advantage. This inner strength becomes a vital ally as you venture beyond the walls of academia into the broader landscape of life, ensuring you are unbothered and willing to face any adversity that comes your way. Here are some additional practices for building resilience through mindfulness:

- Daily Mindfulness Meditation: Start or end your day with a 10-minute mindfulness meditation. Focus on your breath and observe your thoughts without judgment to center your mind, which can enhance emotional flexibility and resilience over time.

- Gratitude Reflection: Keep a gratitude journal where you record things you're thankful for each day. Reflecting on positive aspects of life can shift your mindset from one of deficiency to abundance, reinforcing mental strength.

- Compassionate Self-Talk: Practice speaking to yourself with compassion, especially during challenging times. Mindful self-compassion can transform negative thought patterns into supportive ones, enhancing your ability to bounce back from adversity.

- Mindful Listening: Engage in active listening during conversations, focusing entirely on the other person without planning your response. This enhances your ability to be present and fosters deeper connections, which are vital for resilience.

- Mindfulness Bell: Set periodic reminders on your phone or computer to take brief mindfulness pauses. Use these moments to breathe deeply and center yourself, which can help in maintaining a resilient state of mind throughout the day.

- Mindful Observation: Choose an object in nature and focus on it intently, observing all the details and qualities it possesses. This practice enhances concentration and the ability to focus on the task at hand, a key component of resilience.

- Yoga or Tai Chi: Participate in yoga or tai chi classes, which are physical forms of mindfulness. These disciplines teach you to move with intention and awareness, strengthening the mind-body connection and fostering resilience through physical balance and flexibility.

Each of these strategies intertwines the development of a mindful approach to daily life with the strengthening of resilience. These are all practical tools to navigate stress and recover from setbacks with ease and success. Pick one and start there, or if you've spent college building up your practice already, ask yourself, "How can I double down on my commitment to myself?" Maybe a weekend mindfulness retreat, or even a new yoga mat or meditation stool? You've got options – enjoy this moment!

Embracing Self-Care

After completing your college journey and stepping into the post-graduation phase, staying healthy and active are very important. The demands and uncertainties of life after college can sometimes make it challenging to prioritize your well-being. However, making health and physical activity an important piece of your routine is a crucial aspect of achieving success and happiness.

In the enthusiastic pursuit of your post-college dreams, it's easy to overlook the significance of staying healthy and active. This chapter underscores the importance of a commitment to physical well-being, post-graduation activities, and finding a healthy work-life balance. Regular exercise and an active lifestyle are the building blocks of a healthy life after college. Engaging in physical activities, whether it's through sports, fitness routines, or outdoor adventures, provides numerous benefits, boosting your energy levels, reduces stress, and improves your overall health.

Work-life balance is not complete without an emphasis on maintaining a healthy body and staying active. A strong and energetic physical foundation will empower you to navigate the challenges of your career and personal life more effectively. Your ability to remain active and healthy will greatly contribute to your success and happiness.

The lying down meditation exercise provided in this chapter serves as a symbol of celebration for your achievements, no matter how small. It is a reminder that your journey is not just about reaching the destination but also about cherishing the milestones along the way.

In your quest for success and happiness in the post-college world, remember that mindfulness is a lifelong journey, and it will serve as your steady companion. With mindfulness and a commitment to staying healthy and active, you are well-equipped to face the challenges, seize the opportunities, and create a future that is not only successful but also deeply fulfilling.

Chapter Seven

A Mindful Life

Mindfulness extends far beyond the management of stress and anxiety; it is a way to cultivate a more fulfilling and meaningful life. As Jon Kabat-Zinn describes it, cultivating mindfulness within ourselves and our lives is "the challenge of a life's time," but it is also the "challenge of a lifetime." We "choose to cultivate [mindful] capacities for learning, growing, healing, and transformation right in the midst of our moments." In doing this, we come to know "who we really are" and can trust that we are "living our lives as if they really mattered." The entire experience of a mindful life can be captured in the feeling of gratitude. When a person embarks upon this lifetime challenge of mindfulness, the gratitude in their lives compounds. And gratitude, more than anything else, is the source of joy in our lives. In this section, you will learn how gratitude and mindful living can shift your perspective, enabling you to find joy in everyday moments and build stronger connections with those around you.

Gratitude is a powerful tool for cultivating happiness. Take time each day to reflect on the things you're grateful for, no matter how small. This practice can shift your focus away from what you lack to what you have, fostering contentment and satisfaction.

Life after college unfolds as an ever-flowing stream of decision-making, filled with many possibilities and uncertainties. Each choice, from selecting the ideal job opportunity to weighing personal and financial matters, carries significant weight and potential consequences. It's in this realm of decision-making that mindfulness reveals itself as a treasured guide, offering a distinctive perspective that empowers you to navigate the choices that lie ahead.

Mindfulness is not a quick fix, it is a lifelong practice. As you progress, you'll find opportunities to deepen your mindfulness practice with advanced techniques. Whether you choose meditation, yoga, or mindful walking, this chapter will illuminate the path to making mindfulness an integral part of your daily life.

It can be as simple as taking a few minutes each day to sit quietly, focus on your breath, and observe your thoughts without judgment. Consistency is the cornerstone of mindfulness. We will emphasize the importance of checking in with yourself, not just during challenging moments, but throughout your journey into the post-college world. The goal is to empower you with the tools to manage stress and anxiety, and to adapt to the ever-evolving landscape of life after college.

Right now, mindfulness can be instrumental in managing the transitions and challenges that come with your college life. It offers young adults tools to cope with academic pressure, peer relationships, and the search for purpose. Building and nurturing relationships, including those with partners, children, and extended family, requires patience, empathy, and effective communication. Mindfulness, with a focus on self-awareness and empathy, can enhance these interpersonal skills. It helps individuals remain present in their relationships, fostering deeper connections, and better conflict resolution.

This time in your life often prompts self-reflection and a quest for meaning. Mindfulness can facilitate this process by encouraging introspection. It enables you to better understand your goals, values, and passions. Through mindfulness, individuals can embark on a journey of self-discovery, making more intentional and fulfilling life choices.

In the later stages of adulthood, maintaining physical and mental well-being becomes even more important. Mindfulness practices like yoga and mindful walking promote physical health, flexibility, and mental clarity. They are essential tools for aging adults to stay engaged, maintain cognitive function, and experience a sense of vitality. Mindfulness can even be a valuable companion in the later stages of life when individuals reflect on their existence and prepare for the inevitable. It helps in embracing the present moment, finding peace in the face of uncertainty, and connecting with loved ones during these challenging times. It evolves with each stage of life, offering support, resilience, and a deeper connection to the self and the world. As individuals progress through the different phases of adulthood, mindfulness stands as a valuable and adaptable practice, empowering them to navigate life's complexities easily and with self-awareness.

The transition from college to post-college life is undoubtedly a momentous one, marked by change, challenges, and uncertainties. It is a time when the cheers of graduation day give way to the daunting reality of the future. But it is also a time when mindfulness can shine as a guiding light, helping recent graduates navigate the complex path ahead.

Mindfulness is not an abstract concept but a practical tool that can be integrated into your daily life. It offers strategies to manage stress, cope with rejection, and ultimately lead a more fulfilling and meaningful life. Through the practice of mindfulness, you can develop self-compassion, resilience, and a deeper understanding of yourself. Meditation, self-reflection, and gratitude are just a few of the avenues through which you can deepen your mindfulness practice and find joy in everyday moments.

As you navigate life after college, remember that mindfulness is not just a tool for self-improvement but also a means to connect with others on a deeper level. By empathizing effectively and fostering meaningful relationships, you will find invaluable support and guidance as you continue to grow and evolve.

Chapter Seven

Jordan's Story

Once draped in the comfort of college corridors, Jordan now stood at the crossroads of a daunting world. The diploma, a testament to years of dedication, felt weightless against the uncertainty of a wavering economy. Jobs were plentiful, yet the quality ones – those that sparked a fire in Jordan's heart – seemed unreachable.

Amid this challenge, Jordan's refuge was mindfulness, a practice embraced during the final years of college. It was more than a routine; it was a lifeline, an anchor in the complicated world of post-college life. Each morning, Jordan sat in silence, legs crossed, taking breaths deep and steady. This ritual was not about escaping reality, but instead confronting it with a calm mind and resilient spirit.

The job hunt was a relentless cycle of hope and disappointment. Interviews came and went, each a learning curve, each with one step forward and three steps back. Jordan watched peers settle for less, their dreams sacrificed for that stability. The temptation to follow was strong, but a voice within, honed by hours of mindful reflection, urged patience.

Graduate school emerged as a beacon in the haze of options. It promised advancement, knowledge, and a break from the job market's harsh realities. Yet, it also meant more debt, more years away from the dream of making a tangible impact. Jordan grappled with this decision, the pros and cons swirling in his head.

One evening, amidst this turmoil, Jordan returned to his good ol' college campus. The familiar paths, now lined with the amber hues of sunset, brought a flood of memories and emotions. Sitting under the sprawling oak, a silent witness to Jordan's journey, the answer slapped him in the face. Resilience, Jordan realized, wasn't just about enduring the hardships, but about making choices that aligned with one's deepest values, the motivation for one to keep going. Mindfulness had sharpened this understanding, revealing that the essence of resilience was in the power of informed, conscious decisions.

The decision was made. Jordan would continue the job search, but with a renewed focus. It wasn't about finding just any job, but the right job, one that resonated with the values and aspirations that are developed over years of academic and personal growth. As Jordan stepped into the job market with renewed vigor, each rejection and setback was met with a mindful pause, reminding him that resilience was a journey, not a destination. And in this journey, the lessons of mindfulness – patience, clarity, and inner strength – were his ultimate guidance. In the heart of hardships, where quantity overshadowed quality, Jordan's mindful resilience shined bright, a testament to the power of inner peace in navigating life's ever-present challenges.

Exercise: Lying Down Meditation

Lying down meditation can be a wonderful practice to incorporate into your life. Lying down meditation can be particularly beneficial for relaxation, stress reduction, and body awareness. It can also be an effective way to address physical discomfort, as you're in a position that minimizes strain on your body. If you fall asleep while doing a lying down meditation, go easy on yourself and know that your body is telling you that it needs sleep more than anything else.

Step 1: Choose a Comfortable Location

Find a quiet and comfortable place where you won't be disturbed. It could be a yoga mat, a soft carpet, or your bed. Ensure the room is at a comfortable temperature.

Step 2: Lie Down Mindfully

Lie on your back with your legs extended and arms resting by your sides, palms facing up. Make any adjustments necessary to ensure you're as comfortable as possible. You may want to use a cushion under your head or a blanket to cover yourself.

Step 3: Close Your Eyes

Gently close your eyes to minimize visual distractions.

Step 4: Bring Awareness to Your Body

Start by taking a few deep breaths to center yourself. Then, slowly bring your attention to different parts of your body. Does a particular part of your body feel tired or fatigued? Do you feel fidgety or energetic in one part of your body? Does your arm or leg make an involuntary movement? Notice any areas of tension or discomfort, but try not to judge or change them. Simply observe. Let's take several minutes to do this now.

Step 5: Focus on the Breath

Begin to shift your attention to your breath. Pay attention to the natural rhythm of your breath as it flows in and out. Don't try to change it. Simply

Notice the rise and fall of your abdomen and the sensation of the breath as it enters and exits your nostrils.

Step 6: Non-Judgmental Awareness

Continue to focus on your breathing. If your mind wanders or if you become aware of physical sensations or thoughts, acknowledge them without judgment, and gently guide your focus back to your breath. Maintain your breath awareness for the next several minutes.

Step 7: End with Gratitude

When you're ready to conclude the meditation, slowly bring your awareness back to your breath. As you take a few final deep breaths, express gratitude to yourself for taking this time to nurture your well-being.

Reflection Questions

1. How can you apply these mindfulness practices and principles to your changing environments? How could you have applied these actions to your last transition (think graduating from high school or a time you moved)?

2. How can you create a support system or community of individuals throughout your lifetime to encourage positive self-care and mindfulness practices for yourself?

3. When confronted with setbacks, what mindful strategies might you employ to cultivate resilience and maintain a positive mindset?

4. How can you integrate mindfulness at your workplace to manage stress and improve your overall well-being, and what specific techniques or exercises will you incorporate?

5. In what ways can you apply the principles of mindfulness to enhance your communication and relationships with your coworkers and boss, and what strategies will you utilize to make these principles consistent and long-term?

Common Challenges

Mindfulness, often misconceived as a serene journey, is rightfully termed a 'practice' for its inherent challenges. It's a path marked by hurdles that even the most dedicated individuals face. Recognizing this, we've compiled a list of common challenges encountered in mindfulness practice, accompanied by strategic ways to navigate and overcome them. This guide aims to assist practitioners in transforming these obstacles into stepping stones towards a deeper, more fulfilling mindfulness experience. Remember, the journey of mindfulness is not about perfection, but progress and persistence in the face of these universal challenges.

Fidgeting

In Kabat-Zinn's exploration of mindfulness, the body is described as potentially experiencing discomfort, restlessness, and an array of sensations such as tingling, itching, or compelling urges to move. These sensations, initially debilitating, can be transformed through mindfulness practice. By acknowledging and recognizing them as mere sensations without attaching great significance, the body's discomfort can be held lightly and gently in awareness, akin to any other bodily sensations. This shift in perception reflects the transformative power of mindfulness, allowing individuals to navigate physical discomfort with a heightened sense of presence and acceptance.

Breaking the Silence

Sometimes the mindful silence of meditation can be uncomfortable. With practice, there can be profound acceptance of the body's signals which fosters tranquility amidst potential unease. Kabat-Zinn highlights the collective nature of mindfulness, emphasizing that in moments of meditation, individuals are not alone but connected to a universal, silent "presencing" without bounds. There is difficulty in truly staying silent amid the constant influx of sensory stimuli, but the awareness achieved through silence envelops all audible aspects of existence, underscoring the depth and challenge of sustained mindfulness practice.

Congestion

When you're all stuffed up and can't breathe proper-
ly, meditation might feel like a stretch, breathing becomes more challenging, and it requires more attention than usual. Mindfulness helps us become aware of
these sensations, making us appreciate every breath
— whether it's easy or difficult due to a stuffy nose. It
encourages us to pay attention to our breathing, transforming it from a habit into something we consciously
appreciate for our well-being. If feeling congested, you
don't have to force yourself into a formal meditation
session; instead, it's about gently acknowledging the
sensations and being kind to yourself in the midst of
discomfort due to congestion. One can simply participate in gentle moving or stretching exercises. This can
help ease tension and improve breathing without ex-
erting too much effort.

Distractions (ADD/ADHD)

In the hustle of college life, it's easy to get caught up
in the chaos and lose sight of the present moment. As
Jon Kabat-Zinn reminds us, our ability to pay attention is not just a luxury but a lifeline — a lifeline that
leads us back to the meaningful aspects of our lives
that often go unnoticed in the fast-paced whirlwind of

academia. Learning how to refine our attention and sustain it is like finding the key to unlock a world of significance that might be missed, ignored, or brushed aside in our relentless pursuit of deadlines and goals. It's a challenge to slow down, especially when the pressure is on, but as Kabat-Zinn suggests, embracing the present moment is where true richness lies. So, fellow college students, let's not be reluctant to hit pause, take a breath, and fully immerse ourselves in the now. Through the rhythmic counting of breaths, we might find the missing link to a more fulfilling and balanced college experience.

Lack of Motivation

A diminished sense of motivation can act as a substantial impediment to cultivating a consistent and effective meditation routine. When the desire to engage in meditation wanes, the inclination to prioritize other activities or succumb to distractions becomes more pronounced. Overcoming this obstacle requires a deliberate commitment to rekindle motivation by recognizing its importance in personal well-being. Much like the approach to overcoming drowsiness, addressing a lack of motivation involves understanding that the benefits of meditation extend beyond the immediate and are integral to fostering mental clarity and emotional balance.

By actively acknowledging and navigating through periods of low motivation, individuals can pave the way for a more meaningful and transformative meditation practice.

Drowsiness (Eepy)

When the mind is clouded by sleepiness, maintaining focus and cultivating awareness become more difficult. In meditation, whether seated or lying down, combating the pull of drowsiness is essential for an effective practice. Approaching meditation with a well-rested and alert mind is crucial for unlocking its full benefits. If you fall asleep during a time of meditation, take note of that and ask yourself what needs to change for more effective meditation. Adequate sleep lays a foundation for heightened concentration, making it easier to dive into the depths of meditation with clarity and intention. Prioritizing sufficient rest becomes not just a matter of physical well-being but a strategic approach to creating an environment conducive to a more profound and transformative meditation experience. If the goal is to truly awaken within one's practice and life, then attending to the quality of sleep becomes a fundamental aspect of supporting that intention.

Hunger (Hangy)

In his insightful observation on the essential nature of eating, Jon Kabat-Zinn offers a valuable pro tip. He urges us to consider eating not just as an activity but as a fundamental aspect of life, only second to breathing in its importance for all living organisms. He emphasizes the critical role of eating in sustaining ourselves, highlighting that the innate drives of hunger and thirst must be satisfied daily. This necessity goes beyond mere sustenance; it involves the discrimination of taste, a survival mechanism especially vital in the wild. Kabat-Zinn's perspective underscores the importance of eating as an instinctive, life-preserving act that requires both attention and appreciation while practicing mindfulness throughout the process.

Frustrated (Angy)

In the midst of college's hustle and bustle, here's some mindfulness wisdom to carry with you: encounters with impatience or agitation are not stumbling blocks; they are habitual patterns of thought. Understand them as mere habits of the mind, and let this awareness become a powerful tool. As you navigate the whirlwind of college experiences, don't see moments of anger and impatience as obstacles, but rather as opportunities for growth. Embrace them, integrate them into your meditation practice, and watch them transform into anchors guiding you to deeper self-awareness. In the realm of mindfulness, these challenges are not distractions; they are valuable objects for meditation, paving the way to a more centered and resilient version of yourself.

Authors

Nghi Bùi is from Houston, Texas, where she moved to from Vietnam in 2019. She is attending the Integrated Business and Engineering Honors Program at Lehigh University in Bethlehem, PA. This marks her first published work. Nghi is passionate about exploring diverse cultures, and her time at Lehigh Launch American West has given her opportunities to learn from different perspectives from locals. As she navigates through her education, she is dedicated to learning and exploring as much as possible about the world.

Grace Burns is from Wingdale, New York in the Hudson Valley. This is the first book she has written that has been published. She is attending P.C. Rossin College of Engineering at Lehigh University in Bethlehem, PA, with an anticipated major of Environmental Engineering. She has learned a lot of valuable lessons while working on this book and hopes that it will make a difference for college students like her. A fun fact about her is that she is an avid equestrian, competing in both Hunter Jumpers and Barrel Racing. She also has a very strong passion for spending time outdoors when she is not on the farm. Grace wants to give a shout out to all of her supporting friends, family, and teachers for encouraging her to always do her best.

Authors

Alexandra Chevez is from Houston, Texas, currently attending Lehigh University with an intended marketing major in the College of Business. With a great appreciation for the outdoors, she loves to travel to various national parks and take road trips with family and friends in her free time. Beyond her love for nature, she finds creative expression through the lens, engaging in the art of photography. As a first-generation student, she hopes to inspire others like her and encourage them to fearlessly pursue their ambitions and break barriers.

Adrian Chui is an optimistic author and future engineer with the intention of majoring in engineering physics and electrical engineering at Lehigh University and comes from Philadelphia, Pennsylvania. He graduated from Roman Catholic High School. He has various hobbies, including coding, ice hockey, chess, and musical instruments. He enjoys the understanding and development of technological devices. He has played several different musical instruments, including violin, viola, and oboe. Having a passion for engineering and meditation, he is influenced to write about mindfulness in a captivating way to combine the online and real-world for readers. Adrian wants to thank all the people around him that supported him through his journey and the development of this amazing book. :)

Jackson Clary is from Western Springs, IL and graduated from Lyons Township High School in the class of 2023. He is currently majoring in Business at Lehigh University. Beyond the confines of academic life, Jackson is a multifaceted individual with a diverse range of interests. A sports enthusiast at heart, he actively engages in various athletic activities, finding joy and fulfillment in the competitive spirit of sports. Jackson's love for sports underscores his commitment to a healthy and active lifestyle. In addition to his athletic pursuits, Jackson possesses a keen interest in philosophy, particularly drawn to the principles of stoicism. Delving into the timeless wisdom of philosophy, he explores the teachings that emphasize virtue, resilience, and a rational approach to life's challenges. This interest showcases Jackson's intellectual curiosity and a reflective mindset that extends beyond the bounds of conventional academic subjects.

Sabine Dalais is a student in the P.C. Rossin College of Engineering at Lehigh University. Coming from the small island of Mauritius, she loves snorkeling, kayaking, scuba diving, and learning about marine environments. Part of appreciating nature is about being present in the moment and mindful of all the things occuring around you. She hopes to impart these same skills in readers so that they can apply it to their college experience.

Ivan Gatski is a young author hailing from rural Millville, Pennsylvania. After graduating from Millville High School, he is currently pursuing a major in Mechanical Engineering in the Rossin College of Engineering at Lehigh University. Ivan hopes to one day find employment in the engineering field. In his free time, he can often be found exploring the great outdoors via bicycle. When not cycling, Ivan also enjoys restoring his classic 1986 Ford F150.

Nadxieli Jimenez Bielma is a first generation student from Houston, Texas. Nadxieli is currently a first-year at Lehigh University and is a part of the Integrated Degree in Engineering, Arts, and Sciences (IDEAS) program. This will be her first time publishing a book and incorporating mindfulness into her life. Her goal for this book is to inspire other college students, such as herself, to step out of their comfort zone and to learn how to navigate this new chapter through mindfulness. With this book, Nadxieli would like to bring reassurance to college students that they are not alone on this journey, as she embarks on it herself. Her personal hobbies include playing volleyball, soccer, and baking for those she loves. During this semester out west, she picked up crocheting and is on to her second project!

Carlos Ramos is from the Spring Branch area of Houston, TX. He is attending the P.C Rossin College of Engineering at Lehigh University. He plans on majoring in Mechanical Engineering and Theater. While writing the book he has enjoyed learning more about mindfulness and its benefits. His hobbies include woodworking, working as a crew in theater productions, and designing. After graduation he wishes to work on creating a more sustainable future by helping design more environmentally friendly transportation.

Authors

Zeke White is pursuing an Environmental Engineering degree at Lehigh University's P.C Rossin College of Engineering. He enjoys a variety of outdoor activities, such as rock climbing, white-water paddling, and scuba diving. His passion for the natural world drives him in his pursuit for environmental advocacy and protection, and he hopes to use his new knowledge in promoting the conservation of its beauty.

Audio Exercises

Meditation can be challenging, which is why we've included audio versions of each chapter's mindfulness exercises, brought to you by voiceover artist and ASMR Reiki healer, Kelly Jean Badgley, of the YouTube Channel, *This ASMR Reiki Life*. We encourage you to carve out a few moments in your day, ideally between 15 to 20 minutes, to engage with each exercise. Simply scan the QR code provided here. It will seamlessly direct you to our publisher's website, where you can conveniently download and embark on each exercise individually.

That's Deep. Audio Exercises

These exercises are more than just practices; they're pathways to greater peace, clarity, and inner strength. Trust in the process, and be gentle with yourself as you explore the depths of your mind, body, and spirit. Thank you so much for choosing our book. Your journey towards mindfulness is a deeply personal one, and we are honored to be a part of it.

Exact Rush

Discover More with Exact Rush

If you've enjoyed *That's Deep.* by Lule West, we invite you to explore the world of Exact Rush publications.

Explore Our Range

At Exact Rush, we pride ourselves on a rich selection of titles that focus on spirituality, religion, and identity. From insightful, cerebral non-fiction, to imaginative works that transports you to different realms or teach you something new, our catalog of accurate, informative, and life-affirming titles continues to grow.

Have a Book Idea?

Do you have a story to tell or knowledge to share? Exact Rush is always on the lookout for unique voices and compelling content. If you have a book idea that aligns with our ethos, we would love to hear from you. Our team is dedicated to nurturing and promoting new talent.

Contact Us

Your journey with Exact Rush Multimedia Publishing doesn't end here. To explore our catalog or discuss a book idea, visit **exactrush.com** or contact us at **exactrushllc@gmail.com.** Let's continue to explore, learn, and grow together.

www.ingramcontent.com/pod-product-compliance
Lightning Source LLC
Chambersburg PA
CBHW051416090426
42737CB00014B/2700